new bistro

when I was two, which was my first French experience. Thanks to you both.

New Bistro
by Fran Warde

First published in Great Britain in 2009 by Mitchell Beazley,
an imprint of Octopus Publishing Group Ltd,
2–4 Heron Quays, London E14 4JP
An Hachette UK Company
www.hachettelivre.co.uk

ISBN: 978 1 84533 330 0

A CIP record for this book is available from the British Library.

Set in Adope Garamond and Beerdip
Colour reproduction by Fine Arts in Hong Kong
Printed and bound by Toppan Ltd in China

Note: Bistro recipes may have been adjusted to make them usable in the family home.

Commissioning Editor Rebecca Spry
Art Director Tim Foster
Senior Editor Leanne Bryan
Editor Maggie Pannell
Proofreader Jo Murray
Indexer Isobel McLean
Executive Art Editors Yasia Williams-Leedham
   & Pene Parker
Designer Geoff Borin
Photography Jason Lowe
Production Manager Peter Hunt

Author's acknowledgements
Firstly, I would like to thank France for being a foodie's inspiration, with its copious markets, extraordinary wines and its huge variety of bistros. Thanks also to the French people for not being food snobs; they are clearly passionate about simplicity, seasonality and local produce, and whenever I visit France I come back overjoyed and energized with a new idea, recipe, food item or bottle of wine. This always makes my heart skip a beat and I immediately want to get cooking in the kitchen on my return.

Thanks, too, to all the bistros that have contributed recipes, kitchen skills and stories of their origins and buildings. A big thank you to owners and chefs who explained their recipes at length and helped when back in the UK we had to find alternative ingredients to make recipes work; many a phone call and email later, we arrived at the final, delicious results.

A big thank you to all the following people: the enthusiastic Rebecca Spry for asking me to write this book and for giving me such a wonderful freedom, allowing me to choose bistros that express the range of this huge country; Jason Lowe, who followed in my footsteps to shoot brilliant and stimulating photographs; Maggie Pannell, for her dedicated editing eye, and for never altering anything without a conversation; Yasia Williams-Leedham who, with her high energy and her endless zeal for books, is a delight to spend time with; Geoff Borin, for the beautiful layout, which makes this project visually pleasing and complete; and the lovely Leanne Bryan, whose concluding editing touches on this book bring all the pages together ready for all to read. Also, a big thank you to Michael Alcock, whose wisdom and humour is just dazzling.

Thanks to all my family and friends, who helped keep family life together while I left the boys and travelled over to France on research. There are many of you, but I'd especially like to thank Mum and Dad, Hilary Miller, Nicola and Adam Blackwood, and my tolerant husband David. Thanks, too, to everyone who answered my requests or sent me details of their favourite bistros, especially Didier Foure, Henry Harris and Jane Ryon – who I had not seen for 20 years and then met by chance in Le Lavondou…what a small world.

Thanks to everyone at the Hotel de Toiras in Ile de Ré – a truly beautiful and comfortable place – for their kind hospitality. For more information, call +33 (0)5 46 35 40 32 or visit www.hotel-de-toiras.com.

I finally have to thank my younger son, who ate his way around Lyon and Paris with me and, 2 years later, still talks of each meal in detail!

Fran Warde

new bistro

Including recipes from France's best bistros

Mitchell Beazley

contents

Introduction

Rumour has it that the French word *bistro* (or *bistrot*) originates from 1815, when Russian soldiers captured Paris and walked the streets shouting *bystro* (meaning 'quickly' in Russian) to the waiters as they entered cafés; so *bistro* came to mean a place where 'fast food' was served. Funny, that, as today 'fast food' tends to indicate a rather unpleasant meal cooked en masse and served in polystyrene boxes! Speak to a French person and they consider a bistro to be a place for a drink and maybe a sandwich, nothing more. I believe that it is the romantic traveller visiting France that has given further meaning to the word *bistro* – using it to conjure up a simple but perfectly balanced French meal, using local seasonal produce, served in a quaint environment with charm. It's the memory that we take home from a French holiday and then, in the midst of winter, smile sweetly and dream of perfect bygone days. Today in Paris, bistros are abundant, very good and used by Parisians for lunch and early suppers. Parts of Provence have bistros, and there seems to be a current resurgence. But sometimes one feels for the tourist market, as eateries are more often than not just named for what they are rather than after the style of restaurant, be it a brasserie, auberge, domaine, bistro or even 'Chez' followed by the owner's name. However, they all serve food, whether in the style of a bistro or in true French style.

The preparation and cooking of food is rapidly changing in France and with it come difficulties. Some places stick to their guns and serve what they know best, whereas others are moving with the times and bringing French food into the 21st century – which is a very good and brave thing to do. Some places just supply food for tourists, as in all countries, but this food is not always an authentic representation of French cuisine. It can be hard to find a truly traditional meal in France as a holiday-maker; the best advice is to research before you go (the internet is amazing). All French towns have an *office de tourisme* and this will list restaurants. *The Michelin Guide* is also a brilliant source of information, and gives a quick and concise opinion to restaurants, even if it is a little heavy with very small print! If a restaurant has made it into the guide, it is meant to be good, although sadly from my experience I would not say that this is necessarily true! Always steer clear of the main tourist street, with its restaurants side by side all vying for your attention. The real eating places are generally hidden away in the back streets.

My heart always skips a beat when I find somewhere where the staff do not speak a word of English that is full of French people of all generations eating – this is when I feel that I am in for an authentic French treat and a voyage of food discovery!

One thing that will strike you first of all about eating in France is the quality of staff: in France, waiting is a profession, wine-waiting is a passion and cooking is an art that is taken seriously, both by chefs and home cooks. Take the humble green salad: the French really know how to make a fresh and quick dressing, and this is very often used to dress homegrown, crunchy lettuce leaves. Food can really be as simple as that: it is the simplicity and quality of ingredients that give a meal its fine and perfect balance. At the same time, the French love to eat out. This is part of their culture and it is something that goes much further than eating; it involves testing, questioning, passing judgement, arguing and – obviously foremost – enjoying and savouring the unique cooking of a particular eatery. They enjoy choosing a meal and really know how to get just what they want out of the chef. Many chefs love this, as there is nothing better than cooking for someone who is intelligently opinionated!

France is a massively diverse country surrounded by three different seas, five different countries and the Alps. This regional variation results in distinct local produce and flavours. All good chefs love to cook with local produce and many are passionate about the food of their region. They will generally stick to the local style of cuisine, with the exception of Paris, which, as with all capital cities, offers the full range of the country's cuisine. Paris is one city that does this with real style, and for a city that is not on the coast it has great fresh seafood readily available for all. Be it in a noted bistro or your humble local, they will all, at some time of the week, offer really fresh and delicious oysters that taste unmistakably of the Atlantic.

The French are very proud of their local produce and use it with expertise and knowledge. Every region has its own wine, cheese, herbs, vegetables, fruit and meat or fish speciality, and the French use these ingredients to create the dishes for which they have become world famous. The bistros that I have selected for this book demonstrate the diversity of use of local products, be it Saint-Marcellin sauce in Lyon, *fleur de sel* in the Ile de Ré or sardines in Nice. France is also a very visual country and its people have a wonderful decorative flair. Their style can be either very elegant or fashionably 'shabby chic', which many of us aspire to. My eating environment is very important, and in this book I have selected some very unique bistros, some to showcase the individual style of a particular region, and some to demonstrate the style of the bistro owner. While travelling and eating my way across France, I also met some wonderful people, many of whom inspired me with their knowledge and love of good produce and food, and encouraged me to add in the recipes I'd collected personally on my travels. I would like to thank all the bistros featured, and their owners, without whom this book would not have been at all possible, for sharing their knowledge and recipes and putting up with my 'amusing French' (as one owner kindly described it!).

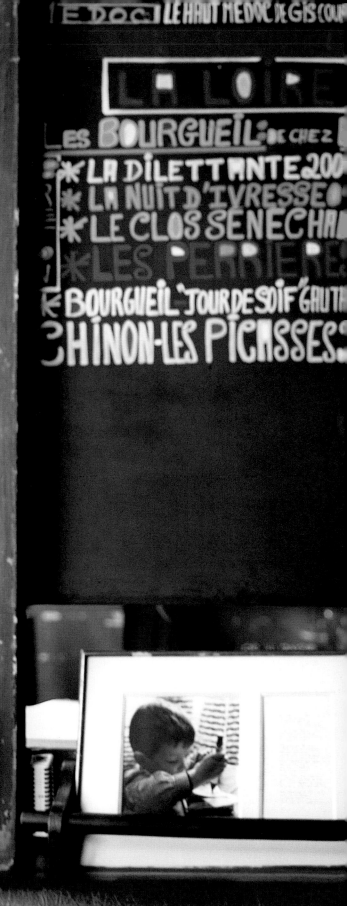

Normandy

This very green and lush part of France is abundant with good produce – pungent creamy cheeses; apples, pears, cherries and *pommeau* (pear cider); fish and seafood, especially oysters from Caen and large blue-shelled mussels; creamy butter and crème fraîche; artichokes; lamb from the salt plains near Mont Saint Michel – the list goes on. It is a cook's heaven. Visit the markets and the stallholders will all be supplying what is in season. They are very proud of their produce and will be keen to tell you about its production or life, and how best to prepare it. That is what I love about the French – they are strongly opinionated about food and are quite happy to share their thoughts and skills, believing every time that their way is the best and they are always right! There is never an inch of doubt in a French person's kitchen. Their self-belief is enormous, and their desire for good food never ceases.

Mariner's mussels

Moules Marinières

On a sunny day overlooking the coast this is the most perfect meal: plump mussels, fresh from the sea, served with a lovely spicy sauce, crusty bread and a crisp green salad.

Preparation: **5 minutes**
Cooking: **20 minutes**
Serves: **4**

50g (2oz) butter

2 tbsp olive oil

3 garlic cloves, crushed

3 shallots, diced

2kg (4½lb) mussels, cleaned and washed

1 red chilli, deseeded and thinly sliced

200ml (7fl oz) white wine

1 bay leaf

sprig of fresh thyme

sea salt and freshly ground black pepper

grated zest and juice of 1 lemon

large bunch of fresh parsley, chopped

fresh bread, to serve

Heat the butter and oil in a large pan, add the garlic and shallots and sauté for 5 minutes without colouring.

Discard any mussels that are even slightly open or damaged and do not close when tapped against the side of the sink.

Add the chilli, mussels, wine, bay leaf, thyme and seasoning to the pan, cover with a lid and cook for 10 minutes, tossing the mussels from time to time to ensure even cooking. The mussels are cooked when they have opened. Discard any that have not opened.

Spoon the mussels out into a large pot using a draining spoon and keep warm.

Return the pan with the cooking liquor to a high heat, boil rapidly for 5 minutes to reduce, then add the lemon zest and juice and chopped parsley.

Pour over the mussels and serve with large quantities of bread.

Spring asparagus with lemon hollandaise

Asperges de printemps à la hollandaise au citron

Lightly cooked asparagus fresh from the fields is perfect served with this lemon hollandaise and will not disappoint.

Preparation: **15 minutes**

Cooking: **2 minutes**

Serves: **4**

24 asparagus young/new season spears, ends trimmed

juice of 1 lemon

2 egg yolks

salt and freshly ground white pepper

125g (4½oz) butter, melted

Heat a large pan of boiling water, plunge the asparagus into it and simmer for 2 minutes until just tender. Drain the asparagus and lay on a clean tea towel to remove any excess moisture.

It is easiest to make the hollandaise sauce with a hand-held blender. Blend the lemon juice, egg yolks and seasoning together in a jug, then slowly pour in the melted butter, blending all the time until you have a glossy, coating-consistency sauce. Place the jug over a pan of hot water to keep it warm.

Serve the asparagus with the warm hollandaise sauce poured over.

Soufflé omelette with goats' cheese and rosemary

Omelette soufflé au chèvre et romarin

Visit any bistro when you're in a hurry and they will always be able to rustle up an omelette and green salad for you. This is a lovely, classic recipe with a unique twist – the airiness of the omelette just melts into the creamy goats' cheese.

Preparation: **5 minutes**
Cooking: **8 minutes**
Serves: **1**

knob of butter

2 eggs, separated

sprig of young fresh rosemary, finely chopped

sea salt and freshly ground black pepper

60g (generous 2oz) soft goats' cheese

Preheat the oven to 180°C/350°F/Gas 4. Melt the butter in a 20cm (8-inch) thick-based frying pan with an ovenproof handle. Whisk the egg whites until stiff, add the chopped rosemary and seasoning, then fold in the egg yolks.

Tilt the pan to ensure the melted butter evenly covers the pan base. Add the omelette mix, tilt the pan to spread it out evenly and cook over a low heat for 5 minutes.

Crumble the goats' cheese on to one half of the omelette, carefully flip over the other half to cover the cheese, then place in the oven to bake for 3 minutes. Serve immediately.

Sole with spinach

Sole aux épinards

Fresh from the sea, wonderful sweet-tasting sole, pan-cooked with fresh spinach make this a treat both for the cook and the friends at your table.

Preparation: **10 minutes**

Cooking: **25 minutes**

Serves: **6**

50g (2oz) butter

2 tbsp olive oil

6 small sole, gutted and skinned

500g (1lb 2oz) fresh spinach, washed and chopped

100ml (3½fl oz) white wine

2 lemons, 1 juiced and 1 cut into wedges

bunch of spring onions, finely sliced

sea salt and freshly ground black pepper

torn fresh coriander, to garnish

Preheat the oven to 180°C/350°F/Gas 4. Divide the butter and oil between two frying pans large enough to take a sole each, heat these, then pan-fry the fish for 3 minutes on each side. Drain and transfer to a lightly oiled roasting tray, cover with foil and place in the oven. Repeat until all the sole are cooked.

Divide the spinach between the two frying pans and cook turning frequently for 2–3 minutes. I like the spinach to be warmed but not wilted, but this is a personal choice – cook for a little longer, if desired. Transfer the spinach on to warm serving plates.

Combine the pan juices in one pan, add the wine and lemon juice and bring to the boil. Add the spring onions and season to taste. Place a sole on top of the spinach on each plate and spoon over the juices. Garnish with the torn coriander and serve with lemon wedges.

Chicken baked in cider

Coq au cidre

This is the Normandy version of **pot au feu,** *using cider rather than stock, with the addition of crème fraîche, to add richness. In Normandy, where this cream is bountiful, it is constantly added to a vast variety of recipes.*

Preparation: **30 minutes**
Cooking: **1 hour 25 minutes**
Serves: **4**

4 shallots, chopped
2 celery sticks, chopped
2 carrots, chopped
2 bay leaves
bunch of fresh thyme
2kg (4½lb) free-range chicken
sea salt and freshly ground black pepper
650ml (1 pint 2fl oz) dry cider
2 tbsp crème fraîche
roughly chopped fresh chervil, to garnish

Preheat the oven to 180°C/350°F/Gas 4. Place the shallots, celery, carrots and herbs in a large casserole or ovenproof baking dish. Place the chicken on top, season and pour in the cider. Cover and bake in the oven for 1 hour.

Remove the lid from the casserole or baking dish and cook the chicken for a further 15 minutes. To test if it is cooked, push a skewer into the thigh at the thickest point. If the juices run clear, it is done; if not, give it another 5 minutes, then test again. Lift the chicken out and keep warm, remove and discard the herbs and strain the cooking liquor into a jug.

Purée the vegetables in a blender until smooth, check the seasoning and keep warm. Pour the cooking liquor into a pan and place back on a high heat. Add the crème fraîche and boil until just thick.

Carve the chicken, spoon over the sauce and serve with the vegetable purée. Garnish with the chervil.

Roast rolled veal loin with sage, lemon and spinach stuffing

Longe de veau à la sauge, citron et épinards farcis

This was cooked for me at a French friend's house for supper while I was travelling around France and writing this book, and it was so good that I had to get the recipe. In homage to her, it should really be called Veau de Jane!

Preparation: **40 minutes**
Cooking: **1 hour 20 minutes**
Serves: **4**

600g (1lb 5oz) veal loin
25g (1oz) butter
200g (7oz) spinach, washed and chopped
2 garlic cloves, crushed
zest and juice of 2 lemons
bunch of fresh sage, chopped
1 tsp Dijon mustard
1 tbsp crème fraîche
sea salt and freshly ground black pepper
6 smoked streaky bacon rashers
200ml (7fl oz) vegetable or chicken stock

Preheat the oven to 160°C/325°F/Gas 3. With a large sharp knife, cut into the loin lengthways and cut round, so turning the loin into a flat sheet. Place the meat between two sheets of greaseproof paper and beat with a mallet until even and flat and measuring about 30 x 20cm (12 x 8 inches).

Melt the butter in a pan, add the spinach and garlic and cook for 3 minutes until wilted. Squeeze out any excess moisture. Place the spinach in a bowl and add the lemon zest, sage, mustard, crème fraîche and seasoning, and mix well.

Spread the stuffing over the flattened veal and roll the meat, taking care to keep the stuffing in at the ends. Wrap the bacon around the outside and tie with butcher's string to keep in place.

Place the rolled veal in an oiled roasting tin and roast in the oven for 1 hour, turning frequently to get the outside golden all over. When it is cooked through, remove the veal from the roasting tin and keep warm.

Place the roasting tin directly over the heat, add the lemon juice and stock and boil rapidly until reduced by one third. Season to taste. Carve the veal into generous slices and serve with the sauce.

Rabbit with sorrel sauce

Lapin à l'oseille

Wild rabbit has a lot more flavour than farmed and both can often be found across France. Rabbit features regularly on bistro menus in the countryside, where it is most probably wild rabbit.

Preparation: **10 minutes**

Cooking: **1 hour**

Serves: **6**

25g (1oz) butter

1 rabbit, cut into portions

1 tbsp plain flour

sea salt and freshly ground black pepper

500ml (18fl oz) chicken stock

1 bay leaf

sprig of fresh thyme

350g (12oz) sorrel, trimmed

2 egg yolks

125ml (4fl oz) crème fraîche

Heat the butter in a large frying pan or flameproof casserole and cook the rabbit pieces on all sides until sealed and golden brown. Sprinkle in the flour and mix to absorb any fat and juices, then cook for 3 minutes. Add the seasoning, stock, bay leaf and thyme, bring to the boil, cover with a lid and simmer for 40 minutes, or until cooked through.

Meanwhile, chop the sorrel roughly and whisk the egg yolks with the crème fraîche.

Remove the cooked rabbit from the pan and keep warm. Remove and discard the bay leaf and thyme sprig. Add the sorrel to the cooking juices, mix and cook for a further 2 minutes.

Add a few spoonfuls of the cooking juices to the egg mixture and blend, then pour into the pan and stir constantly over a very low heat for 5 minutes, until the sauce thickens just enough to coat the back of a spoon. Do not boil. Return the rabbit to the pan to warm through and serve coated with the sauce.

Leek and potato soup with crispy bacon

Vichyssoise au bacon

I have a very strong image imprinted on my mind, after travelling through France, of French shoppers returning home from their local market with all their fresh produce, and every basket containing a large, green cluster of leeks. This soup tastes best when you make it using homemade chicken stock made from the carcass of a roast.

Preparation: **10 minutes**

Cooking: **40 minutes**

Serves: **6**

500g (1lb 2oz) leeks, trimmed and sliced

1 tbsp olive oil

250g (9oz) potatoes, peeled and diced

1 litre (1¾ pints) chicken or vegetable stock

sea salt and freshly ground black pepper

6 thinly sliced smoked bacon rashers, halved widthways

100ml (3½fl oz) crème fraîche

bunch of fresh chervil, chopped

truffle oil (optional)

Place the leeks in a large pot with the oil and sauté for 5 minutes without browning. Add the potatoes to the leeks, cook for a further 4 minutes, then add the stock and seasoning and simmer for 30 minutes.

Liquidize the soup in a blender or food processor or, for a truly smooth texture, pass the soup through a fine potato mill. Return the soup to the pan, check the seasoning and adjust if necessary.

Grill the bacon slices until crispy and golden. Serve each bowl of soup topped with a teaspoonful of crème fraîche, two pieces of crispy bacon and a scattering of chopped chervil. Add a few drops of truffle oil, if liked, for a truly memorable soup.

Stone fruit and crème fraîche cake

Gâteaux aux fruits et crème fraîche

In the summer months, when fresh apricots, nectarines, cherries and peaches are abundant and you want to cook with them, why not make this lovely dessert-style cake to enjoy with a fine cup of coffee?

Preparation: **20 minutes**

Cooking: **25–30 minutes**

Serves: **4–6**

115g (4oz) butter, softened, plus extra for greasing

115g (4oz) brown sugar

2 eggs

5 tbsp crème fraîche

200g (7oz) stone fruits (such as apricots, nectarines, cherries and peaches), halved, stoned and chopped

125g (4½oz) self-raising flour

¼ tsp baking powder

½ tsp grated nutmeg

Preheat the oven to 180°C/350°F/Gas 4. Grease a 20cm (8-inch) round cake tin. Blend together the butter and sugar until evenly mixed. Add the eggs and beat vigorously, then add the crème fraîche and chopped fruits and mix. Quickly fold in the flour and baking powder until smooth.

Transfer the cake mixture to the prepared cake tin, dust with grated nutmeg and place in the oven to bake for 25–30 minutes. To test whether the cake is cooked, insert a fine skewer into the centre – it should come out clean with just a few crumbs attached. Allow the cake to cool in the tin for 5 minutes before turning it out on to a wire rack. Serve cut into slices.

Pancakes with sticky apples and pears in Calvados

Crêpes Normandes

Wickedly indulgent and loved by anyone with a sweet tooth, this is my variation on simple pancakes with butter-fried apples, pears and caster sugar. This is delicious served with a scoop of vanilla ice cream.

Preparation: **15 minutes, plus 30 minutes resting**

Cooking: **45 minutes**

Serves: **6**
(makes 12 small pancakes)

115g (4oz) plain flour
300ml (½ pint) milk
1 large egg
2 dessert apples
2 dessert pears
115g (4oz) caster sugar
40g (1½oz) butter
100ml (3½fl oz) double cream
2 tbsp Calvados (optional)
melted butter, for brushing pan

Place the flour in a bowl, whisk the milk and egg together, then slowly mix into the flour, whisking until smooth. Cover and leave the batter to rest for 30 minutes.

Cut the fruit into wedges and remove the cores. Carefully heat the sugar in a pan over a low heat until it forms a golden caramel. Remove from the heat and add the butter and cream – this will splatter and go lumpy at first, but if you mix it well it will soon become smooth. Add the prepared fruit and Calvados, if using, mix to coat the fruit, then set aside keeping the mixture warm.

Brush a 20cm (8-inch) frying pan with the melted butter and heat. Add a small ladleful of batter and tilt the pan to make it spread thinly and evenly. Cook for 1–2 minutes, flip with the help of a spatula and cook for a further 1 minute. Transfer the cooked pancake on to a warm plate and repeat until all the batter is used, brushing the pan with a little more melted butter as needed between pancakes.

Serve the pancakes folded over with some of the sticky fruits inside.

Bistrot les Quatre Chats
8 rue d'Orléans
14360 Trouville-sur-Mer

Tel +33 (0)2 31 88 94 94

Owners: Serge and Muriel Salmon

*Open 12noon Friday, Saturday and
Sunday, and 7.30pm Thursday –
Monday*

*Closed Monday, Tuesday and Wednesday
lunchtime and evening, and Thursday
lunchtime*

Closed 20 November – 20 December

Bistrot les Quatre Chats

Wander away from the waterside restaurants and weave your way around the maze of old streets to find this remarkable, lively and unique eatery owned by husband and wife Serge and Muriel Salmon, who have a passion for love, ginger and laughter. All this shines through in their bohemian bistro. They met 19 years ago and both worked in busy jobs in Paris, but they always knew that one day they wanted to have their own restaurant. They arrived in Trouville-sur-Mer 15 years ago, rented the ground floor of a scruffy shop and opened Bistrot les Quatre Chats. Today the bistro spans three floors and they own the entire building!

The menu changes every day and is chosen by Muriel, the chef. It is dictated by the seasons and by the perfect balance of flavours that are *acidulé* (sour, or sharp) and sweet. Muriel is self-trained; her grandfather and father both loved cooking but for this smiling chef, it is a passion. Her food is not classically French as she loves to play around with recipes and add different spices and flavours, delivering constant surprises. This bistro is a play in motion!

During the Deauville Film Festival, a studio company takes over this huge, colourful and characterful bistro for private parties, and the 'A' list of Hollywood has sat on its multi-coloured railway carriage seats. This is a happy place with two very loving and enthusiastic owners.

Langoustine flans with cream and saffron sauce

Flan de langoustines, et sa crème au safran

The luscious, rich and creamy flavours of Normandy help create this easy yet sophisticated seafood starter. If you can't source langoustines, replace them with prawns.

Preparation: **30 minutes**

Cooking: **1 hour**

Serves: **6**

300g (10oz) raw, shelled langoustine tails

3 eggs

325ml (11fl oz) crème fraîche

6 drops Tabasco sauce

salt and white pepper

Cream and saffron sauce

300ml (½ pint) double cream (unpasteurized if possible)

pinch of saffron strands

Preheat the oven to 110°C/225°F/Gas ¼. Chop the langoustine tails. Beat together the eggs, crème fraîche, Tabasco and seasoning, then stir in the chopped langoustines. Lightly butter 6 individual ramekin dishes and divide the mixture between them using a ladle.

Place the ramekins in a bain-marie (a large pan or roasting tin filled with boiling water, coming about two thirds of the way up the sides of the ramekins) and cook in the oven for 1 hour. Do not attempt to speed the cooking up by putting the oven on a higher heat. When cooked, the flans should be just firm to the touch.

While they are cooking, make the cream and saffron sauce. Gently heat the cream and saffron in a pan for 3–4 minutes – the cream will turn a pale orange colour.

When the flans are cooked, turn them out on to serving plates and spoon over a little saffron sauce. Serve immediately.

Crab and chilli crusties

Croustillants de crabe au piment

Preparation: **30 minutes**

Cooking: **15 minutes**
**(5 minutes for each tray
of filo triangles)**

Serves: **6**

**500g (1lb 2oz)
white crabmeat**

**1 fresh green chilli, deseeded
and finely chopped**

4 spring onions, finely sliced

**3 sheets filo pastry (keep
wrapped until ready to use)**

85g (3oz) butter, melted

**115g (4oz) spicy salad leaves,
such as mustard, watercress
and wild rocket**

Mayonnaise
**2 egg yolks
(at room temperature)**

2 tsp French mustard

**sea salt and freshly ground
black pepper**

250ml (9fl oz) sunflower oil

juice of ½ lemon

1 tbsp white wine vinegar

*Delicious, large, fresh crabs are readily available along this
northern coast of France. This recipe mixes the crabmeat
with lovely hot onion and chilli flavours, then stacks it
between crispy filo pastry.*

First make the mayonnaise. Beat the egg yolks in a bowl with the
mustard and seasoning, slowly drizzle in the oil, whisking all the
time, then finally beat in the lemon juice and vinegar. Preheat
the oven to 180°C/350°F/Gas 4.

Place the crabmeat in a bowl, add the chopped chilli, spring onions
and mayonnaise and mix well.

Brush one sheet of the filo pastry with melted butter on both sides
and cut into 6 triangles, measuring approximately 7cm (3 inches)
on each edge. Place on a baking sheet and bake for 5 minutes
until golden. Repeat with the remaining 2 sheets of filo to make
18 baked triangles.

Just before serving, divide the salad leaves between 6 plates. Place
a filo triangle on each salad, add a spoonful of the crab mixture,
another triangle of filo followed by crab, then a final filo triangle
to make stacks. Serve at once before the pastry becomes soggy.

John Dory with lime

Saint-Pierre au citron vert

Preparation: **20 minutes**

Cooking: **1 hour**

Serves: **6**

300g (10oz) celeriac, peeled and chopped

2 carrots, chopped

1 courgette, thickly sliced

4 spring onions, sliced

1 preserved lemon, finely chopped

1 fresh green chilli, finely chopped

5cm (2-inch) piece fresh root ginger, grated

2 pinches of saffron strands

1 litre (1¾ pints) fish stock (*see* below)

salt and white pepper

bunch of fresh coriander, chopped

6 x 200g (7oz) John Dory fillets, bones reserved

lime wedges, to serve

Fish stock

John Dory bones, from filleting

1 onion, roughly chopped

1 bay leaf

2 white peppercorns

1.2 litres (2 pints) cold water

John Dory is a tasty and firm fish, perfect for this very healthy and flavoursome dish containing Muriel's beloved Asian flavours, which work brilliantly. If you're not confident enough to fillet the John Dory yourself, ask your fishmonger to do so and to reserve the bones for you.

First make the fish stock. Place the fish bones, onion, bay leaf and peppercorns in a pan with the water. Bring to the boil, then reduce the heat, cover and simmer for 15 minutes. Strain and set aside. Preheat the oven to 190°C/375°F/Gas 5.

Place the celeriac, carrots, courgette, spring onions, preserved lemon, chilli and ginger in a large roasting tin. Add the saffron to the measured fish stock, season with salt and white pepper, then pour over the vegetables. Cover with greaseproof paper and cook in the oven for 30 minutes.

Add the coriander to the vegetables and stir through. Lay the fish fillets on top, cover again with greaseproof paper and return to the oven for a further 7 minutes, or until the fish is tender.

Remove the fish fillets from the roasting pan and keep warm. Ladle out the vegetables and cooking liquor into serving bowls and top each serving with a fish fillet. Serve with lime wedges.

Raspberries in rose-scented jelly

Framboises en gelée de rose

A dessert for those hot summer days when you fancy something soft and fragrant, but not too sweet. Rose syrup can be found in Middle Eastern shops, but you can use rose water if this is not available.

Preparation: **10 minutes**

Cooking: **5 minutes, plus 3 hours setting**

Serves: **6**

125ml (4fl oz) hot water

2 sachets gelatine (about 11g each)

750g (1lb 10oz) raspberries

4 tsp rose syrup or rosewater

450ml (16fl oz) water

Pour the hot water into a small bowl, add the gelatine and stir briskly until dissolved. If the gelatine does not thoroughly dissolve because the water has cooled, stand the bowl in a pan of warm water over a low heat to help it along.

Divide the raspberries between 6 pretty glasses. In a pan, warm the rose syrup or rosewater with the water, then remove from the heat, add the dissolved gelatine water and stir until blended. Pour over the raspberries and chill in the fridge for 3 hours or until set.

Paris

Paris, France's much-loved capital city, is a melting pot of all the different foods of France. If you want *fruits de mer*, visit one of the *écailleurs* on the city's streets, who will shuck and present you with a fresh and vast array of seafood on a large metal plate filled with crushed ice. Underneath will lie a small plate with shallot vinegar, Tabasco sauce, bread and good butter. Nowhere else does this taste as good to me; it is my staple diet every time I visit the city. There are also places serving sauerkraut from the Alsace region, or a rich and bubbling cassoulet or crispy *confit de canard* from the south-west. Anything is possible in Paris, as with most major cities nowadays, but it is still necessary to seek out good food. This can take a little skill as there are many tourists, so you should always do some research on the internet, check out the great many recommendations and also travel with a good guide – *The Michelin Guide* is a superb all-rounder.

Paris is packed with lovely restaurants, bistros and brasseries. Nothing beats a small, compact bistro offering a great menu of the day, whose ingredients have been bought fresh from the market and then cooked into fabulous but simple classics, such as French onion soup, coq au vin or tarte tatin. In no two places will these dishes taste the same as every chef has a unique way of doing things. Paris just oozes food; there is a food market every few streets, amazing cheese shops, traditional butchers, trattorias selling beautiful, handmade savoury terrines, tarts and prepared seafood timbales and, of course, bakeries and chocolate shops galore! It is very difficult to visit Paris and not to indulge in a bistro or two!

Capital salad

Salade de la Capitale

This is my personal choice of salad. In every bistro you get various salads that are the house or chef speciality. If I owned a bistro, this is the salad I would serve to my diners!

Preparation: **20 minutes**

Cooking: **20 minutes**

Serves: **4**

300g (10oz) waxy, firm-fleshed salad potatoes

4 eggs

200g (7oz) smoked lardons or streaky bacon, chopped

olive oil, for frying

1 head of escarole or frisée lettuce, separated and washed

bunch of fresh chervil

200g (7oz) artichoke hearts (canned or freshly prepared)

Vinaigrette dressing

2 tsp Dijon mustard

1 garlic clove, crushed

2 tbsp red wine vinegar

sea salt and freshly ground black pepper

4 tbsp olive oil

Cook the potatoes in simmering water for 20 minutes, or until tender, then drain and slice. Meanwhile, heat another pan of water and, when just simmering, add the eggs. Bring to the boil for 30 seconds, place a lid on top then remove from the heat and leave to sit for 6 minutes. Rinse in cold water and, when cool enough to handle, shell the eggs.

Fry the lardons or streaky bacon in a pan with a scant amount of oil, until golden.

For the dressing, put the mustard, crushed garlic and vinegar in a large salad bowl, blend well and season. Slowly drizzle in the olive oil and whisk to blend.

Tear the lettuce leaves and half the chervil into the vinaigrette and toss well. Add half the potatoes, the artichoke hearts and lardons and toss again. Roughly tear the soft-boiled eggs in half and place on top of the salad. Season to taste and scatter with the remaining chervil before serving.

onion soup

Soupe à l'oignon

Every region and bistro across France has its own version of this classic. Some use white wine, others red, some slice the onions thickly and others thinly, but this is my version and I find that the marriage of flavours makes a great onion soup! It's best to use white onions as their sweeter-tasting flavour works well in this soup.

Preparation: **25 minutes**

Cooking: **55 minutes**

Serves: **4**

1 tbsp olive oil

6 white onions, finely sliced

2 garlic cloves, crushed

25g (1oz) flour

750ml (1 pint 7fl oz) beef stock

250ml (9fl oz) red wine

sea salt and freshly ground black pepper

4 slices French bread

100g (3½oz) Gruyère cheese, grated

bunch of fresh chives, snipped, to garnish

Heat the oil in a medium pan, add the onions and garlic and sauté gently for 30 minutes. Then increase the heat and sauté for a further 5 minutes, allowing the onions to take on a golden colour.

Add the flour and mix in well, then slowly pour in the stock and wine, season and bring to the boil. Reduce the heat, cover and leave to simmer for 20 minutes, stirring from time to time.

Toast the bread, top with the grated cheese, then grill until melted. Serve the soup topped with the Gruyère toasts and garnished with a sprinkling of chives.

Roquefort and pear tarts

Quiche Roquefort et poire

The classic French quiche is world famous and this recipe was a delicious variation that I once ate in Lille at a very unpretentious little eatery. Boy was it good! I recommend using either Williams or Dorée pear varieties for their luscious flavour.

Preparation: **40 minutes, plus 15 minutes for chilling the pastry**

Cooking: **1 hour 10 minutes**

Serves: **4**

Pastry

175g (6oz) plain flour

100g (3½oz) butter

1 egg, beaten

Filling

2 eggs

125ml (4fl oz) single cream

freshly ground black pepper

3 pears, peeled, cored and thinly sliced

150g (5oz) Roquefort cheese

To make the pastry, rub the flour and butter together until the mixture resembles breadcrumbs, add the beaten egg and bind the pastry together to form a ball. Wrap in cling film and place in the fridge to chill for 15 minutes.

Preheat the oven to 180°C/350°F/Gas 4. Roll the pastry out on a floured surface and use to line a 20cm (8-inch) tart tin. Prick the base with a fork and line with baking parchment and baking beans. Place the pastry case in the oven and bake blind for 20 minutes. Remove the baking parchment and beans and bake for a further 15 minutes. Remove the cooked pastry case from the oven.

Reduce the oven temperature to 160°C/325°F/Gas 3. For the filling, beat the eggs and cream with pepper to season (no salt is necessary as the Roquefort is quite salty). Add the pears to the egg mixture and crumble in the Roquefort. Pour the mixture into the pastry case and spread the ingredients out evenly. Place in the oven and bake for 35 minutes, or until just set.

Braised partridge and Puy lentil pot

Perdrix aux lentilles du Puy

Partridges are hunted throughout France and are a much-loved game bird. This method of cooking them brings out the best of all the different ingredient flavours. Puy lentils are famous in France; they are a beautiful colour with a slightly sweet taste and I particularly love them as they keep their individual shape and do not disintegrate with cooking.

Preparation: **15 minutes**

Cooking: **1 hour 10 minutes**

Serves: **4**

2 tbsp olive oil

1 red onion, diced

2 garlic cloves

125g (4½oz) smoked lardons or streaky bacon

500g (1lb 2oz) Puy lentils

200ml (7fl oz) red wine

1 bouquet garni

4 partridges

sea salt and freshly ground black pepper

25g (1oz) butter

2 carrots, sliced

100ml (3½fl oz) water

4 celery sticks, halved lengthways

4 spring onions, trimmed

bunch of fresh parsley, chopped, to garnish

Preheat the oven to 180°C/350°F/Gas 4. Heat the oil in a large, low-sided ovenproof casserole, add the onion, garlic and lardons or streaky bacon and gently sauté until soft. Add the lentils, wine and bouquet garni, then add enough water to cover the lentils. Place the partridges on top, season and cover with a lid. Cook in the oven for 1 hour, or until cooked through.

Meanwhile, heat the butter in a pan, add the carrots and sauté for 5 minutes. Add the water, celery and spring onions and bring to the boil.

Remove the partridge from the oven, increase the oven temperature to 220°C/425°F/Gas 7 and add the sautéed vegetables and juices to the casserole, around the partridge. Return the uncovered casserole to the oven for 10 minutes. Serve the partridge on top of the lentils and vegetables, spoon over any cooking juices and garnish with chopped parsley.

Scallops with spinach and lemon vinaigrette

Coquilles Saint-Jacques aux épinards et vinaigrette au citron

When you next see some large, plump, gleaming scallops at your local fishmonger's, gather them and serve this fantastic, simple dish that I once enjoyed on my travels in France.

Preparation: **15 minutes**

Cooking: **10 minutes**

Serves: **4**

1 tbsp olive oil

16 king scallops, cleaned

sea salt and freshly ground black pepper

300g (10oz) young spinach, thoroughly washed

1 garlic clove, crushed

1 fresh red chilli, deseeded and finely chopped

juice and grated zest of 1 lemon

75ml (2½fl oz) white wine

40g (1½oz) butter

bunch of fresh chives, snipped, to garnish

Heat the oil in a non-stick frying pan and sear the seasoned scallops on each side for 1 minute. Remove from the heat and keep warm.

Add the spinach, garlic and chilli to the pan and toss over a high heat for 3 minutes until the spinach is just wilted. Add the lemon zest, stir, then remove the spinach to a dish and keep warm.

Add the lemon juice, wine and butter to the cooking pan and whisk on a high heat to reduce by half. Serve the spinach on plates, top each portion with 4 scallops and spoon over the sauce. Garnish with a sprinkling of chives.

Roasted veal kidneys with mustard

Rognons de veau sauce moutarde

Veal kidneys are superb and need very little cooking, like a fillet steak. If this is not to your liking, cook for a little longer. Do take care, though, as once overcooked they become a little tough.

Preparation: **10 minutes**
Cooking: **10 minutes**
Serves: **4**

4 veal kidneys
1 tbsp olive oil
20g (scant 1oz) butter
1 shallot, diced
100ml (3½fl oz) white wine
100ml (3½fl oz) chicken stock
2½ tbsp Meaux mustard
sea salt and freshly ground black pepper

Trim the kidneys of any fat or skin, cut in half and remove the central sinewy bits. Heat the oil in a frying pan, add the butter and, when the butter is foaming, add the kidneys. Cook for 2–3 minutes, turn and cook for another 2–3 minutes, then remove from the pan and keep warm.

Drain off the excess fat from the pan, add the shallots and sauté for 2 minutes until soft. Pour in the wine and chicken stock and boil rapidly until the liquid has reduced by half. Add the mustard and stir through to blend.

Slice the kidneys thinly, sprinkle with salt and pepper, then serve with the sauce spooned over.

Coeur à la crème with strawberries

Coeur à la crème et fraises

The consistency of these little heart-shaped desserts will vary depending on the sort of cream cheese you use. Generally, the fresher the cheese is, the softer and lighter in flavour it will be.

Preparation: **15 minutes, plus overnight chilling**

Serves: **4**

300g (10oz) fresh, soft cream cheese

250ml (9fl oz) double cream

85g (3oz) caster sugar

1 vanilla pod

500g (1lb 2oz) strawberries, finely sliced

1 tbsp icing sugar

Line 4 heart-shaped *coeur à la crème* moulds with very fine muslin, which ensures an easy release when you turn them out to serve. (These speciality moulds have holes in the base and are available from good kitchenware shops.)

Beat the cheese until smooth, lightly whip the cream until it just holds its form, then add to the cheese with the caster sugar and blend. Cut the vanilla pod in half lengthways, scrape out the seeds, add these to the cheese, then mix through. Spoon the mixture into the dishes and cover with greaseproof paper. Place in the fridge to chill overnight.

Toss the strawberries in the icing sugar. Turn out the desserts and serve with the sugared strawberries.

Chocolate orange pots

Pots au chocolat et orange

These are delicious little pots of dense, rich chocolate. The orange zest adds a citrus flavour that marries so well.

Preparation: **15 minutes, plus 2 hours setting**

Serves: **6**

200g (7oz) dark chocolate, broken into pieces

300ml (½ pint) double cream

grated zest of 2 oranges

Put the chocolate and cream into a heatproof bowl, place over a pan of simmering water and leave on a gentle heat until the chocolate has melted. Do not allow to boil.

When the chocolate is smooth, stir in the grated orange zest, reserving a little for decoration. Pour into little pots and leave to cool and set for a minimum of 2 hours. Decorate with reserved orange zest to serve.

Benoit
20 rue St Martin
75004 Paris

Telephone +33 (0)1 42 72 25 76

Owner/chef: Alain Ducasse

Head chef: David Rathgeber

*Open daily 12.30 – 2pm and
7.30 – 10.30pm*

Closed bank holidays

Benoit

Remove yourself from the hustle and bustle of central Paris and enter the supreme calm and vintage sophistication of Benoit, which has been here since 1912. It was owned by the Petit family for three generations, but they sold it in 2005 to the master chef Alain Ducasse. The head chef at Benoit is the youthful David Rathgeber, who cooks bistro food with exact precision. Here the quality, preparation, taste and presentation are of the utmost importance. This place is a real treat and you will not be disappointed. Benoit is packed with individuality; a maze of small rooms with highly polished brass and gleaming glass, elegant charger plates, fine silverware and glasses...but this is where the glitz stops. The food is classic bistro cuisine cooked with care and attention. There are two chefs working front of house presenting house pâtés and tarts, and a multitude of waiters, in traditional dress, serving at tables with great warmth and ease.

This bistro has a saying, *'Chez toi Benoit, on boit, festoie, en rois'* ('Come over to Benoit and once you're in, you'll drink and feast just like a king').

Snails in their shells with garlic and herb butter

Coquilles d'escargots au beurre à l'ail et fines herbes

If you buy live snails, they need to be purged before use. Place them in a large bowl with 1 tablespoon of salt and 3 tablespoons of vinegar. Stir well, cover with a lid with a weight on top and soak for 3 hours, stirring occasionally. After this time, wash the snails well in cold water, rinsing three times, to remove all the gunge they produce.

Preparation: **45 minutes, plus 3 hours for purging (if using live snails)**

Cooking: **15–18 minutes**

Serves: **4**

24 large Bourgogne snails (or 24 large ready-prepared Bourgogne snails and their empty shells)

300g (10oz) unsalted butter

25g (1oz) fine mixed herbs (parsley, tarragon, chervil and chives)

6 garlic cloves, crushed and chopped

50g (2oz) fresh parsley, finely chopped

1 shallot, finely diced

salt and freshly ground black pepper

85g (3oz) fresh breadcrumbs

If preparing your own snails, heat a large pan of water then, when boiling, add the snails and simmer for 5 minutes. Drain, refresh in cold running water, then, when cool, remove the snails from their shells, using a small skewer or hat pin and discarding the small black part at the end of the tail. (If you buy cultivated snails they do not need boiling – proceed directly to the second paragraph of the method.)

Preheat the oven to 180°C/350°F/Gas 4. Gently fry the snails in 20g (¾oz) of the butter, add the mixed herbs and a quarter of the garlic, stir and place to one side.

In a bowl, mix the remaining butter to a soft consistency with the parsley, the remaining garlic, the shallot and seasoning. Place some of this herb butter in each snail shell, then insert a snail and more butter, filling just to the top. Finish with a pinch of breadcrumbs.

Place the shells in a snail baking dish, breadcrumb side up, and bake for 8–10 minutes. Serve immediately.

Breton turbot braised in Champagne with crayfish

Turbot de Bretagne braisé au Champagne et écrevisses

Preparation: **40 minutes**

Cooking: **2 hours 10 minutes**

Serves: **6**

1 turbot about 6kg (12lb), gutted

115g (4oz) butter

Stock

50g (2oz) salted butter

115g (4oz) white button mushrooms, sliced

115g (4oz) shallots, sliced into large rings

3 garlic cloves, crushed in skins

350ml (12fl oz) Champagne

sprig of fresh parsley

3 peppercorns

100ml (3½fl oz) olive oil

fleur de sel

freshly ground black pepper

Crayfish

24 large orange-legged crayfish

olive oil, for drizzling

5 garlic cloves, crushed in skins

30ml (1fl oz) fine brandy

sprig of fresh parsley

This recipe is not for the faint hearted; it is for the more experienced cook, but needs to be included as it demonstrates the diversity of bistro cooking. To help you on your way in the kitchen (unless you are a dab hand at preparing fish) instruct and watch your fishmonger prepare the turbot into gleaming white, trimmed turbot steaks. Ask to keep all the trimmings, except the guts, for the stock.

Clean the turbot, then cut off the head, tail and all the fins and set aside. Skin the fish on both sides and cut into 6 even-sized steaks, about 250g (9oz) each. Using sharp scissors, cut back to the joint of the vertebrae on each side. Cover the steaks and chill them in the fridge.

Start preparing the sauce by first making the stock. Sweat the reserved fish fins in a pan with the butter. Add the mushrooms, shallots and garlic and sweat for 2 minutes. Add the Champagne, cover and simmer for 45 minutes. Remove from the heat, add the parsley and peppercorns and leave to infuse for 20 minutes.

Meanwhile, prepare the crayfish. Preheat the oven to 200°C/400°F/ Gas 6. Separate the heads of the crayfish from the tails, then place the tails only in a roasting pan with a drizzle of oil and roast for 3 minutes. Remove from the oven and add the garlic, brandy and parsley, cover with a damp, clean tea towel and leave to infuse for 15 minutes. Meanwhile, shell the crayfish tails.

Strain the fish stock through a sieve lined with muslin, then heat gently to reduce by one third. Add the oil, season with *fleur de sel* and black pepper and keep warm.

Champagne sauce

**85g (3oz) carrots,
cut into sticks**

**115g (4oz) white button
mushrooms, sliced**

**115g (4oz) shallots,
sliced into rings**

3 garlic cloves, crushed

1 tsp dried fennel seeds

5 black peppercorns

400ml (14fl oz) Champagne

4 egg yolks

salt, to taste

75ml (2½fl oz) clarified butter

juice of ½ lemon

Garnish

24 asparagus spears, trimmed

splash of olive oil

**about 500ml (18fl oz)
chicken stock**

Melt the 115g (4oz) butter in a heavy-based, wide shallow pan, add the turbot steaks and cook until just firm. Remove and place to one side. For the Champagne sauce, place the carrots, mushrooms, shallots, garlic, fennel seed and peppercorns in the pan and heat for 3 minutes. Return the turbot to the pan, pour in half the Champagne and bring to a simmer. Cover and gently simmer for 15 minutes until the fish is just cooked. Lift the turbot out again to rest. Drain the cooking liquor through a sieve lined with muslin into the pan of prepared fish stock.

For the garnish, sweat the asparagus in a pan with the oil and a little salt. Moisten with just enough chicken stock to cover and simmer for 5 minutes. Roll the asparagus in their cooking juices to ensure that they are evenly covered.

Gently warm the fish stock in the pan used for the turbot, then remove it from the heat and add the egg yolks and a few grains of salt. Return the pan to a very low heat and whisk the sauce continuously until it has just thickened. Add the clarified butter and whisk rapidly until emulsified. Finally, add the lemon juice and the remaining Champagne and whisk the sauce over a low heat.

To serve, place the turbot on large warm plates, glaze with some Champagne sauce and garnish with the crayfish tails and asparagus spears. Serve with the rest of the sauce separately in a sauceboat.

Upside-down apple tart

Tarte tatin

David Rathgeber's recipe for tarte tatin will not disappoint. His pre-cooking of the apples ensures that they end up being totally engulfed in the rich juicy caramel.

Preparation: **45 minutes, plus overnight resting time for the pastry and 2 hours chilling for the tart**
Cooking: **1 hour 15 minutes**
Serves: **4**

200g (7oz) caster sugar
4 firm eating apples

Pastry
60g (2¼oz) butter, at room temperature
60g (2¼oz) icing sugar
15g (½oz) ground almonds
½ egg
125g (4½oz) plain flour

First make the pastry. Beat the butter, icing sugar and almonds together, add the egg and beat again. Sift in the flour and mix, roll into a ball, then wrap in greaseproof paper and leave to rest overnight in the fridge.

Preheat the oven to 160°C/325°F/Gas 3. Put the sugar in a 16cm (6¼-inch) diameter ovenproof frying pan and heat carefully over a low heat until it forms a golden caramel. Leave to cool. Peel and core the apples and cut in half from top to bottom.

When the caramel has set, arrange the apples in the pan, rounded-side down, cover with foil and place in the oven. The cooking time varies according to the amount of water in the apples and the rate of absorption into the caramel, so cook until the fruit is soft and the caramel coloured, about 30 minutes. Remove from the oven and leave to cool.

Roll out the pastry on a lightly floured surface into a circle the size of the pan. Push the apples down to make them even on top, cover with the pastry and bake for about 40 minutes, until the pastry is just golden.

Remove the pan from the oven and carefully place in a pan of ice to stop the caramel cooking. Chill in the fridge for 2 hours.

To finish, reheat the pan over a high heat, turning it clockwise for 2 minutes, which gives a lighter and more even touch of heat to help warm and release the tart without burning the caramel. Then place the tart in the oven at 160°C/325°F/Gas 3 for 5 minutes to warm through. Turn out upside down on to a serving dish and serve at room temperature.

Restaurant Astier
44 rue Jean-Pierre Timbaud
75011 Paris

Telephone +33 (0)1 43 57 16 35

restaurant.astier@wanadoo.fr

Owner: Frederick Hubig

Chef: Benjamin Bajolle

*Open daily 12.15 – 2.15pm and
7.30 – 10.30pm*

Restaurant Astier

Slightly off the beaten track in République, away from the central tourist hot spots, this place is a real neighbourhood bistro. It is full of French office workers and little elderly ladies chattering over hearty lunches. It's a simply furnished room – dark wood, traditional checkered tablecloths and enormous napkins with classic bistro cutlery and glasses. It's a warm, noisy, slightly cramped but atmospheric place filled with diners who obviously feel very comfortable there, know just what they want and that it will be cooked well. The kitchen is on the same level as the dining room and, when I was there, I loved the sounds of sizzling, chopping, rustling and steaming, and the general happy chatter that rang through from the kitchen. Every time a dish was ready a little bell would tinkle for a waiter.

The pickled herrings are served in a large pot with a dish of boiled potatoes and you can just help yourself! The turbot is really fresh and perfectly cooked and the *pot au feu* comes in its own dish with an abundance of vegetables. This bistro is famed for its cheeseboard, which is generous and full of a great variety of perfect-quality cheeses.

Astier was established in 1956 by a husband and wife team who had a very unique style of cooking; they took only the very best produce, then cooked it simply but classically to produce great feasts. The bistro has just changed hands and Frederick, the current patron, wants to carry on this tradition with chef Benjamin Bajolle at the helm in the kitchen. The menu is displayed on a blackboard and includes a daily set menu. Every three months a leading item that is in season, such as pig, lamb or rabbit, is designated the speciality of the house and is cooked in every way imaginable for that period. Frederick is passionate about wines and Astier has over 400 wines on its wine list. The staff will be happy to help you if you feel a little overwhelmed by the choice. This is a lovely, gentle, traditional, unfussy bistro that serves fine-quality dishes.

Herrings with potato salad

Harengs marinés avec salade de pommes Rosevalt

Rich herring fillets swathed in oil and served with potatoes is a classic bistro dish. The French, smooth-skinned La Ratte is a good variety of potato to use as it holds its shape well on boiling, but any waxy variety, such as Belle de Fontenay (also French), Charlotte or Pink Fir Apple are also good choices.

Preparation: **25 minutes, plus 12 hours soaking and 12 hours marinating**

Cooking: **about 18 minutes**

Serves: **6**

500g (1lb 2oz) herrings, filleted

milk, to cover herrings

500ml (18fl oz) grapeseed oil

1 clove

5g (¼oz) peppercorns

1 star anise

2 bay leaves

sprig of fresh thyme

1 onion, thinly sliced

1 carrot, thinly sliced

400g (14oz) waxy potatoes

mustard vinaigrette, to serve

Soak the herring fillets in milk overnight or for 12 hours. Drain and discard the milk.

Lay the herrings in a clean, shallow dish, pour over the oil and add the spices, bay leaves and thyme. Place the onion and carrot in a layer on top, cover and leave to marinate in the fridge for 12 hours.

Cook the potatoes in their skins for 18 minutes or until tender. Cool and cut into 1cm (½-inch) slices.

Serve the potatoes with a mustard vinaigrette spooned over and the marinated herring fillets.

Pollack fillets with Parisian sauce

Dos de lieu à la Parisienne

Pollack, or black cod, is fished from the Channel and is an inexpensive but tasty fish that is often used in bistros.

Preparation: **10 minutes**

Cooking: **30 minutes**

Serves: **6**

50g (2oz) butter

400g (14oz) white button mushrooms, thinly sliced

1 carrot, thinly sliced

200g (7oz) celeriac, thinly sliced

6 pollack fillets, about 200g (7oz) each

snipped fresh chives, to garnish

Parisian sauce

3 shallots, finely chopped

250ml (9fl oz) white wine

250ml (9fl oz) single cream

Preheat the oven to 150°C/300°F/Gas 2. Melt half the butter in a pan and sauté the sliced mushrooms, carrot and celeriac for 8–10 minutes. Keep warm.

For the Parisian sauce, put the shallots in a saucepan with the white wine, simmer and reduce by one third. Stir in the cream and simmer again to reduce by one quarter. Strain the sauce and keep warm.

Melt the remaining butter in a large, ovenproof frying pan and fry the fish, on the skin side, for 3 minutes. Then place the fish in the oven to roast for 5 minutes. (Transfer the pollack to an ovenproof dish if the frying pan cannot be used in the oven.)

To serve, top the sautéed vegetables with the pollack, spoon over the Parisian sauce and garnish with a sprinkling of chives.

Sweetbread terrine

Terrine de ris de veau

The addition of mushrooms to this classic terrine, makes it individual to Astier. This is a great example of how a good bistro makes a dish its house speciality.

Preparation: **1 hour, plus 3 hours marinating**

Cooking: **1 hour**

Serves: **6**

115g (4oz) gammon

115g (4oz) roasting veal

200g (7oz) roasting pork

100ml (3½fl oz) port

100ml (3½fl oz) white wine

115g (4oz) veal sweetbreads

25g (1oz) butter

salt and freshly ground black pepper

85g (3oz) horn of plenty mushrooms, chopped

100ml (3½fl oz) double cream

pinch of cayenne pepper

vinaigrette or tarragon mayonnaise, to serve

Chop the gammon, veal and pork into small cubes. Place the meats in a shallow dish, pour over the port and white wine, then cover and leave to marinate in the fridge for 3 hours. Drain.

Preheat the oven to 150°C/300°F/Gas 2. Place the sweetbreads in a pan of cold water and bring to the boil, blanching them. Drain and refresh with cold water. Peel and discard the outer membrane from the sweetbreads, then slice them.

Melt the butter in a pan and sauté the sweetbreads with seasoning for 2 minutes on each side. Set aside to cool.

Mix the mushrooms with the marinated meats, cream, cayenne pepper and seasoning.

In a terrine dish, layer the mixed meats and the sweetbreads in alternate layers until all are used. Cover with foil. Place the terrine in a bain-marie (a large pan or roasting tin filled with boiling water, coming about two thirds of the way up the sides of the terrine) and cook in the oven for 1 hour.

Cool the terrine and turn it out of the dish. Serve cut into 1cm (½-inch) thick slices with a little vinaigrette or tarragon mayonnaise (*see* Cook's tip, below).

Cook's tip
To prepare tarragon mayonnaise, mix together 3 teaspoons of tarragon mustard with 3 tablespoons of mayonnaise.

Eggs in 'snow'

Oeufs à la neige aux éclats de pralines, crème Anglaise pistache

Soft, marshmallow-like meringues sitting in a pond of **crème Anglaise** *and then drizzled with sweet caramel make this a marriage of gentle flavours and creamy textures. This is a Parisian classic and, when executed properly, is a real treat. Benjamin adds pistachio paste to his* **crème Anglaise**, *which gives the dish an unusual twist, but was voted 'out' in my house! I love the method of cooking the meringue. It is perfect, easy and works every time.*

Preparation: **20 minutes**

Cooking: **15 minutes**

Serves: **6**

Crème Anglaise

15g (½oz) pistachio nuts (optional)

4 large egg yolks

115g (4oz) caster sugar

500ml (18fl oz) milk

Meringues

4 large egg whites

pinch of salt

160g (5½oz) icing sugar

Caramel

50g (2oz) caster sugar

3 dsp water

10g (scant ½oz) crushed pink pralines, to decorate (optional)

First, make the *crème Anglaise*. Crush the pistachios, if using, in a food processor to make a paste. Mix the egg yolks and sugar in a heatproof bowl for 5 minutes. Bring the milk to the boil in a pan. Off the heat, pour the milk into the beaten egg mixture and stir with a wooden spoon. Return this to the pan and, over a very low heat, stir constantly for about 10 minutes until the mixture thickens, but do not allow to boil. Stir in the pistachio paste, if using, then strain the custard through a fine sieve and cool.

Now make the meringues. Using an electric mixer, whisk the egg whites with the salt until white and stiff. Add the sugar and whisk. Divide the mixture between six unlined ramekins (do not fear they will not come out) and microwave in a 650–700 watt microwave oven for 40–50 seconds until pillow-soft, like marshmallows. Leave to cool.

To make the caramel, heat the sugar in a pan with the water until it turns into a light caramel. Remove from the heat and cool.

Divide the *crème Anglaise* between 6 dessert dishes. Place a snowy meringue in the centre of each and drizzle over a trail of cold caramel sauce and, if using, a sprinkling of crushed pralines.

Ile de Ré

In 1988 a spectacular, 3km-long, arching toll bridge was built over the sea to take people from the mainland and deliver them to this sleepy but popular white-sanded island. Ile de Ré is rich in seafood, especially oysters, and has an abundance of salt flats. The result is that almost every shop on the island sells *fleur de sel de l'Ile de Ré*.

The island has two sides: the sheltered west side has calm, flat seas, whereas the east side offers large, rolling waves from the Atlantic and is a windy paradise for wind and kite surfers. The food on the island is good as many people from Paris visit for holidays and weekends, so a high standard is demanded. Oysters, which are produced on the island, are served abundantly here, and a huge variety of excellent-quality fresh seafood is on offer in all the restaurants. Of all the places I've visited in France, this is where I have eaten the best seafood, and it comes straight from the fisherman's boat to the kitchen. To complement the fish, the island also produces a good crop of potatoes that have their own AOC, salad leaves, herbs and soft fruits. Vineyards, which are found all over the island, make simple red, white and rosé *vins de pays* that are mostly produced by co-operatives, and the island also has its own distinctive, slightly spicy, dark mahogany Cognac. In the high summer months the Ile de Ré teems with cyclists meandering their way through the many vineyards.

Sautéed clam salad with wine and parsley dressing

Salade de palourdes sautées au vin et persil

If you see fresh-from-the-sea clams on sale, snap them up and make this simple summer recipe that is packed with sunshine and the delicious sweet-salty flavours of the sea. Great served with sourdough bread.

Preparation: **25 minutes**

Cooking: **20 minutes**

Serves: **4**

1kg (2lb 4oz) clams

25g (1oz) butter

100g (3½oz) lardons or diced streaky bacon

2 shallots, chopped

1 garlic clove

100ml (3½fl oz) dry white wine

300g (10oz) rocket, washed

bunch of fresh parsley, chopped

sea salt and freshly ground black pepper

First purge the clams. Fill the sink with cold water, add the clams, stir around and leave to soak for 10 minutes. Drain and repeat with fresh water until all the sand is washed out of the clams. Place in a colander and leave to drain for 5 minutes. Discard any clams that are even slightly open or damaged and do not close when tapped against the side of the sink.

Heat the butter in a large, shallow pan, add the lardons or diced streaky bacon and cook until golden. Reduce the heat, add the shallots and garlic and gently sauté for 5 minutes until soft. Add the white wine and clams, increase the heat and cook with a lid on the pan for 5 minutes, until all the clams are open. Discard any that have not opened.

Using a draining spoon, remove the clams from the cooking liquor. Increase the heat and reduce the liquor by half.

Place the rocket in a large bowl, add the clams, parsley and seasoning and toss through the leaves. Pour over the reduced cooking juices, toss again and serve immediately.

Skate wing with lemon butter and capers

Aile de raie au beurre citron et câpres

Skate has always been thought of as a poor man's fish, but due to its growing popularity the price has now crept up. In the summer, serve this with a crisp, green salad; in the winter, serve with creamy, saffron-mashed potatoes.

Preparation: **12 minutes**

Cooking: **12 minutes**

Serves: **4**

100g (3½oz) unsalted butter

4 x 200g (7oz) skate steaks, skinned and trimmed

1 tbsp capers

juice of 2 lemons

salt and freshly ground black pepper

bunch of fresh parsley, chopped

bay leaves, to garnish

lemon halves, to serve

Melt half the butter in a large frying pan, add the skate steaks and cook over a medium heat for 5 minutes on each side. (Depending on the size of the pan, you may need to cook the steaks in two batches.) When cooked, transfer to a dish and keep warm.

Add the remaining butter to the pan and, when foaming, add the capers, lemon juice and seasoning. Stir and bring to the boil. Add the chopped parsley.

Spoon the sauce over the top of the skate wings, garnish with bay leaves and serve with lemon halves.

Cook's tip

To prepare saffron-mashed potatoes, boil floury potatoes until soft, then pass through a sieve or potato ricer. Heat a little milk, add a pinch of saffron and seasoning and beat into the potato until it is smooth and creamy.

Ile de Ré potatoes with crème fraîche and chives, with pan-fried bass

Pommes de terre primeur de l'Ile de Ré et bar grillé

The Ile de Ré is famous for its small, sweet, waxy, golden potatoes, which go so well with a simple sea bass fillet. This is summer food at its best and recipes using both of these local ingredients can be found in many bistros across the island in this season.

Preparation: **10 minutes**

Cooking: **about 20 minutes**

Serves: **4**

300g (10oz) Ile de Ré *primeur* **(first earlies) potatoes, (Ratte or Belle de Fontenay)**

bunch of fresh chives, snipped

1 small red onion, diced

100g (3½oz) crème fraîche

sea salt and freshly ground black pepper

2 tbsp olive oil

4 x 200g (7oz) sea bass fillets

Steam the potatoes whole for 20 minutes until tender. Insert a knife to check that they are soft in the middle. Mix the chives and red onion with the crème fraîche and seasoning.

While the potatoes are cooking, heat the oil in a pan and cook the sea bass fillets for 4 minutes on each side.

Slice the potatoes while still hot and mix with the crème fraîche and chive mixture. Serve with the sea bass.

Strawberry puff pastries

Tarte feuilletée aux fraises

French bistros make beautiful tarts and these always reflect the seasons and the availability of local fruit, so when the strawberry season is in full flow you will see strawberry tarts on the menu. The difference with this recipe is that it uses puff pastry, which is deliciously delicate and flaky, and which marries so well with the soft strawberry texture.

Preparation: **1 hour, plus 15 minutes for chilling the pastry**

Cooking: **25 minutes**

Serves: **4**

Puff pastry

200g (7oz) plain flour

150g (5oz) cold butter, cut into small cubes

125ml (4fl oz) ice-cold water

Filling

250ml (9fl oz) double cream

85g (3oz) ground almonds

500g (1lb 2oz) strawberries, hulled and sliced

1 tbsp icing sugar, for dusting

Sift the flour into a large bowl, then rub in half the butter until the mixture resembles breadcrumbs. Add the water and, using a flat-bladed knife, bring the mixture together to make a dough ball.

Lightly dust a cold working surface and roll out the pastry to a rectangle measuring about 8 x 25cm (3¼ x 10 inches). Dot with half the remaining butter, over two thirds of the pastry length, fold the pastry into three and seal the edges using the rolling pin. Turn the pastry 90 degrees and roll out to the same size. Repeat the process using the remaining butter, roll out and fold, wrap in cling film and place in the fridge to chill for 15 minutes. Preheat the oven to 220°C/425°F/Gas 7.

Unfold the pastry and roll out again to 8 x 25cm (3¼ x 10 inches). Flake the edges using a sharp knife by making a series of shallow cuts horizontally into the pastry, so it resembles the pages of a closed book – this helps the pastry to separate and rise in delicate layers. Place on a lightly buttered baking sheet and cook for 15 minutes, check and reduce the temperature to 180°C/350°F/Gas 4, and then cook for a further 10 minutes. Remove and cool on a wire rack.

For the filling, lightly whip the cream, add the ground almonds and blend until smooth. Spread on top of the cooked pastry, not quite to the edges. Arrange the strawberries on top of the almond cream, dust with sifted icing sugar and serve.

L'Avant Port
8 quai Daniel Rivaille
17410 Saint Martin de Ré

Tel +33 (0)5 46 68 06 68

Owners: Michel and Nagat Azemar

Chef: William Warnault

Open Lunch 12noon – 2pm

Dinner 7pm – when last customer leaves!

*Closed 15 November – 20 December
and 25 – 31 December*

L'Avant Port

Walk away from the main rush of Saint Martin de Ré and over the little island and, next door to the harbour office, near a quiet stretch of houses whose fronts are covered with roses and beautiful hollyhocks, you will find L'Avant Port. This place is new and has only just opened, yet it is bustling with locals and visitors alike. The main room combines the modern and the old: thick stone walls contrast with an entire wall of glass at the back of the bistro, and each table is unique. This is the closest thing I have seen to a British gastro pub in France. It is a joy to be here as the room is lovely, and the view on to the harbour and of the buildings across the way is so pretty.

The chef, William Warnault, has a very clear and simple way of cooking. Instead of gas stoves, his kitchen sports a central island of stainless steel with huge plates for cooking on. These heat up from underneath and a little olive oil is brushed over. Fish is cooked directly on the stainless steel – this cooking method is called *à la plancha*. If you read the menu you find that almost all the food served here is cooked *à la plancha*. The results are amazing: my queen scallops were just perfect: sealed golden on the outside, yet tender and juicy in the middle. Due to this fast method of cooking, all the ingredients that are used have to be really fresh. Fish comes directly from the fisherman, Jean Mark, and the menu is written daily, according to the catch.

Sauces are not really featured here, but your fish may be served with a scant drizzle of green olive oil and a handful of locally grown leaves. Meat comes directly from the AOC producers in the Limousin region, where it has been selected for quality and taste. Three small vegetable producers grow all the herbs and vegetables used at L'Avant Port, and these are collected daily by the owners Michel and Nagat Azemar. You will never see a more beautiful woman than Nagat, who is a Moroccan Berber and just exudes calm elegance and smiles while serving your table. Michel's image when conceiving this new restaurant, was the 'marriage of food, wine and art in a perfect setting'. I think this couple have produced a remarkable place.

Mackerel tartare in anchovy oil

Tartare de maquereaux et anchois à l'huile

This is such a great way of updating mackerel and, when you have fresh fish straight from the sea, it is a real treat to be able to eat it raw and enjoy the clean, fresh flavours. If you want to make more of a meal from this dish, serve it with some steamed Ratte, or another firm-fleshed, waxy variety of potato, tossed in a little olive oil and dill.

Preparation: **15 minutes, plus 1 hour marinating**

Cooking: **15–20 minutes**

Serves: **4**

400g (14oz) skinned mackerel fillets

1 shallot, diced

1 small carrot, diced

2 tsp capers, plus extra to garnish

½ red onion, diced

juice of 1 lemon

sea salt and freshly ground black pepper

2 red peppers, roasted and peeled

50g can anchovy fillets in oil, drained, oil reserved

bunch of fresh basil

Finely dice the mackerel fillets. Add the shallot, carrot, capers, red onion, lemon juice and seasoning and mix together well. Cover and leave to marinate in the fridge for at least 1 hour.

Carefully cut the red pepper flesh into 8 small oval shapes. Finely dice 4 of the anchovies, then cut the remaining anchovy fillets into thin strips.

Using a 10cm (4-inch) chef's ring, make a neat, round portion of the mackerel mixture on each serving plate. If you do not have a ring just spoon the mixture neatly on to the plates. Garnish the tartare with pieces of the cut red pepper, strips of anchovy, diced anchovy, a few capers, basil leaves and a drizzle of anchovy oil.

Baby squid with red pepper stuffing

Chipirons farcis aux poivrons rouges

This is a great way to present this abundant seafood and pack in some extra flavour. Serve this dish on its own or on top of some fresh garden leaves and hot chopped chilli.

Preparation: **30 minutes**

Cooking: **25 minutes**

Serves: **4**

20 squid, each 10cm (4 inches) long

4 tbsp olive oil, plus extra for oiling the roasting tin

50g (2oz) cured ham fat preferably Parma, diced

1 small onion, chopped

3 shallots, chopped

1 red pepper, deseeded and chopped

1 garlic clove, crushed

1 fresh red chilli, deseeded and chopped

bunch of fresh flat-leaf parsley

salt and freshly ground black pepper

250ml (9fl oz) white wine

Clean the squid: pull the tentacles from the body and remove and discard the clear quill, rinse the body, cut the bulbous part off the tentacles and discard, then rinse the tentacles.

Heat half the oil in a pan and quickly sauté the tentacles on a high heat for 4 minutes, stirring constantly. Remove from the heat and allow to cool. Heat the ham fat in the pan, add the onion, shallots, pepper, garlic and chilli and sauté on a medium-low heat for 5 minutes. Preheat the oven to 180°C/350°F/Gas 4.

Place the sautéed vegetables in a food processor with the parsley, seasoning and cooked tentacles and blend until evenly chopped. Stuff the mixture into the cleaned squid either by using a small spoon or by filling a piping bag with the mixture and piping the filling into each squid. Lay the stuffed squid in a lightly oiled roasting tin, roll to coat in oil and cook in the oven for 10 minutes.

Remove the cooked squid from the roasting pan and keep warm. Deglaze the pan: place the pan directly on the hob, add the white wine and simmer rapidly to reduce by half. Add the remaining olive oil and mix, then serve the cooked squid with the reduction spooned over the top.

Hake parcels with vegetables

Croustillants de merlu et julienne de légumes

The sautéed, buttered vegetables in this dish go so well with this lean, almost fat-free fish. Wrapping them in filo pastry with the hake and then baking the pastry parcels in the oven locks in all the delicious flavours.

Preparation: **25 minutes**

Cooking: **12–15 minutes**

Serves: **4**

4 x 200g (7oz) hake fillets

40g (1½oz) butter

2 carrots, 2 leeks, 1 celeriac, and 2 parsnips, each cut into fine julienne

1 tsp ground cumin

salt and freshly ground black pepper

4 sheets filo pastry

2 tbsp olive oil

4 tsp Dijon mustard

Preheat the oven to 200°C/400°F/Gas 6. Place the hake on a couple of sheets of absorbent kitchen paper, place some more sheets on top and pat with your hands. This removes any excess moisture and helps keep the pastry parcels crispy.

Melt the butter in a large pan, add the vegetables, cumin and seasoning and sauté for 3 minutes.

Lay one sheet of filo pastry out and brush with a little oil. Brush one hake fillet with 1 teaspoon of the mustard and place in the middle of the sheet of pastry. Add a quarter of the sautéed vegetables and fold the pastry over the fish, making a parcel with the pastry ends underneath. Brush the outside of the pastry parcel with a little oil and place on a baking sheet. Repeat until all 4 parcels are prepared.

Place the parcels in the oven and bake for 7–8 minutes until the pastry is golden and crispy and the fish has cooked through. Serve immediately.

LE FEU DE BOIS

Les Entrées

Harengs Pommes à l'huile 6,50€
Croustillant de Chèvre chaud 7€
Mouclade charentaise 11€
Terrine de Canard 7,50€
Foie Gras au Torchon 14,50€
Bulots Aïoli 9€
Mousseline 3 Poissons 7,50€
Crumble Tomates & Parmesan 10€
Sardines crues marinées 8,50€
Assiette de la Mer 14€

LES HUITRES

          n°4   n°2
x 6:   7€   10€
x 9: 10,50€ 14,50€
x 12: 14€   19€

Cbrépinette 2€

Assiette de Fromage

LES PLATS

Marmite du Pêcheur 20€
Bar Grillé 20€
Plat du Marché 17€
Blancs de Seiche Grillés 16€
Ballotine de Daurade 14€
Thon rouge à la Confiture d'Oignons 18€
Andouillette de Troyes grillée 12,50€
Entrecôte grillée 17€
Confit de Canard 13€

LES DESSERTS

Dessert du Jour
Fromage blanc au
Oeuf à la Neige
Baba Cool 7€
Prumeaux au
Poire pochée au Cara
la Fleur
Tarte au citron me
Croquant au Chocol
Glaces & Sorbe

HARENGS SAURS
FILETS de HARENGS SAURS
MORUE SALÉE
FILETS DE MORUE

INCOMPARABLE

La Cabane du Fier
Le Martray
17590 Ars en Ré

Tel +33 (0)5 46 29 64 84

Chef: Christopher Frigière

Open 1 May – 31 October

Lunch 12noon – 2pm

Dinner 7 – 10pm

*Closed Monday lunchtime and
all day Wednesday*

La Cabane du Fier

Drive through the centre of the Ile de Ré towards the north of the island and you come across an oyster farmer's cabin with this lovely bistro attached to it, serving seafood in what can only be described as a cabin with a strong tented-structure attached. The view across the flat oyster beds on the east side of the island is amazing. This is Fiers d'Ars – a really beautiful, slightly haunted landscape.

The interior is eclectic and varied: there are lots of old cooking utensils, boating artifacts, tea and coffee pots, and ceramic birds on all the tables. It's a mismatch, and yet it actually works in this environment. There is also a notice that reads 'the objects that you can see may be for sale!' All I can hear is laughter and the sound of cutlery on plates and, for some reason, both noises ring around the rooms adding to the warmth and the joie de vivre of good food. The food is hearty, robust and tasty with chef Christopher Frigière in charge of the kitchen. Every day a blackboard is chalked up displaying the menu of the day, and the choice is large, with an abundance and variety of tempting seafood dishes – I do not think that it's possible to find fresher oysters!

Tomato crumble

Crumble de tomate

This is a great dish for late summer or early autumn when tomatoes are abundant. Christopher uses cumin to season his tomatoes; I prefer a teaspoon of chopped mixed fresh herbs, but I'll leave you to make your choice. When basil is abundant and in season, Christopher likes to serve this dish with a small glass of chopped basil mixed with Parmesan, garlic and a little fromage frais.

Preparation: **20 minutes**
Cooking: **40 minutes**
Serves: **4**

850g (1lb 14oz) tomatoes
1 tbsp olive oil
1 red onion, thinly sliced
2 garlic cloves, crushed
sea salt and freshly ground black pepper
¼ tsp ground cumin or 1 tsp chopped mixed herbs (*see* recipe introduction)
115g (4oz) cold butter
150g (5oz) flour
115g (4oz) Parmesan cheese, finely grated

Preheat the oven to 200°C/400°F/Gas 6. Make a nick in the skin of each tomato, plunge into a bowl of boiling water for 12 seconds, remove and, when cool enough to handle, peel, then slice.

Heat the oil in a large pan, sauté the onion for 5 minutes until soft, then add the garlic and tomatoes and bring to a simmer. Cook for about 10 minutes, or until all the excess liquid has evaporated, then season and add the cumin or mixed herbs.

In a bowl, rub the butter and flour together until it resembles breadcrumbs. Stir in the grated Parmesan.

Put the tomato mixture in a shallow baking dish and evenly sprinkle over the crumble mix until it is all used. Bake for 25 minutes until golden and bubbling.

House salad

Salade de la Cabane

*A lovely, gutsy salad without a trace of Marie Rose sauce...
but it does contain a naughty spoonful of tomato ketchup!*

Preparation: **30 minutes,
plus 45 minutes cooling**

Cooking: **8 minutes**

Serves: **4**

1 onion, diced

**1 green pepper,
deseeded and diced**

**1 red pepper,
deseeded and diced**

1 tbsp olive oil

125g (4½oz) queen scallops

125g (4½oz) peeled prawns

**125g (4½oz) white cuttlefish,
sliced**

2 garlic cloves

**sea salt and freshly ground
black pepper**

1 tbsp tomato ketchup

½ tsp coriander seeds, crushed

juice of 1 lemon

2 tomatoes

bunch of fresh basil

125g (4½oz) salad leaves

Gently sauté the onion and peppers in the oil for 4 minutes.
Add the scallops, prawns, cuttlefish and garlic, cook for a further
4 minutes, then season. Add the ketchup, crushed coriander seeds
and lemon juice. Mix well, then remove from the heat. Cool and
chill in the fridge.

Make a nick in the skin of each tomato, plunge into a bowl of
boiling water for 12 seconds, remove and, when cool enough to
handle, peel away the skins. Cut into quarters, cut away and discard
the core and seeds, then dice the tomato flesh.

Tear the basil leaves and add to the fish salad, keeping a few small
leaves for garnishing. Divide the salad leaves between 4 plates and
top with a spoonful of the fish mixture. Scatter over the diced
tomatoes and reserved basil leaves and serve.

Grilled white cuttlefish

Blancs de seiche grillés

Cuttlefish are related to squid but tend to be larger. The sea around the Ile de Ré has many, so they are often on the area's bistro menus. Replace with squid if they are not available locally, and smile at your fishmonger and ask him to prepare them for you. If preparing them yourself, follow the method in the recipe for Baby squid with red pepper stuffing (see page 74). Ratatouille and sauté potatoes make good accompaniments to this dish.

Preparation: **10 minutes, plus 1 hour marinating**

Cooking: **6 minutes**

Serves: **4**

850g (1lb 14oz) cuttlefish or large squid

2 tbsp olive oil

sea salt and freshly ground black pepper

lemon wedges, to serve

Cut the squid bodies open and lightly score the flesh in a crisscross pattern. Rub the bodies and tentacles with the oil and season. Cover and leave to marinate for 1 hour.

Preheat a grill or barbecue to a high heat and cook the squid for 3 minutes on each side. Serve with lemon wedges.

Fish stew from the Charente

Chaudrée Charentaise

This must be the most simple fish stew that I have ever come across. I suppose this is all down to the quality of the produce; it's so good that the dish can remain uncomplicated and still delight. Next time you pass an abundant fish counter, buy some fish and treat yourself to this lovely stew.

Preparation: **25 minutes**

Cooking: **30 minutes**

Serves: **4**

400g (14oz) potatoes

2 tomatoes

400g (14oz) mussels, cleaned and washed

250g (9oz) courgettes, thickly sliced

2 onions, thinly sliced

4 x 125g (4½oz) pieces turbot fillet

4 x 125g (4½oz) bass fillets

125g (4½oz) raw langoustines

200ml (7fl oz) white wine

2 dsp olive oil

sea salt and freshly ground black pepper

85g (3oz) cold butter, cut into small pieces

large bunch of fresh parsley, chopped

Preheat the oven to 180°C/350°F/Gas 4. Boil the potatoes in their skins for 10 minutes then, when cool enough to handle, peel each potato and cut into about 4 slices.

Make a nick in the skin of each tomato, plunge into a bowl of boiling water for 12 seconds, then remove and, when cool enough to handle, peel, deseed, then chop.

Discard any mussels that are even slightly open or damaged and do not close when tapped against the side of the sink.

Spread the potatoes, courgettes and onions in a large ovenproof dish, arrange the fish and shellfish over the top, then add the tomatoes, wine, olive oil and seasoning. Cover and bake for 15 minutes.

Remove the stew from the oven and lift out the fish and vegetables on to hot plates. Discard any mussels that have not opened. Pour the cooking liquor into a pan and bring to the boil. Add the pieces of butter and whisk vigorously to emulsify, making a thin sauce. Pour over the fish and serve sprinkled with the chopped parsley.

Poached pears with fleur de sel caramel sauce

Poires pochées au caramel et à la fleur de sel

This recipe is simply divine, believe me! I love the caramel sauce and the pears poached in a vanilla syrup, all topped with a few chopped hazelnuts. Christopher serves his with a scoop of pear sorbet – but I love it on its own.

Preparation: **15 minutes, plus 20 minutes cooling**
Cooking: **25 minutes**
Serves: **4**

500ml (18fl oz) water
500g (1lb 2oz) caster sugar
1 vanilla pod, split lengthways
4 conference pears (fairly firm), peeled, cored and left whole
4 scoops of pear sorbet
4 strawberries, halved, to decorate
4 sprigs of mint, to decorate
chopped hazelnuts, to decorate

Fleur de sel caramel sauce
50g (2oz) caster sugar
25g (1oz) butter
2 tbsp crème fraîche
pinch of *fleur de sel*

Place the water in a pan with the sugar and vanilla pod and heat until a syrup is formed. Carefully place the pears in the syrup and put a round of greaseproof paper on top of them weighted down with a wooden spoon – this helps to keep the pears submerged in the syrup. Simmer the pears for 20 minutes, then remove from the heat and leave to cool in the syrup.

To make the caramel sauce, gently dissolve the sugar in a small heavy-based, non-stick pan until it forms a golden caramel. Remove the pan from the heat and leave to cool for 5 minutes, then add 2 tablespoons of the pear cooking liquor, the butter, crème fraîche and a pinch of *fleur de sel*. Mix well to blend and leave to cool.

Spoon the poached pears into shallow dishes, pour over the liquid caramel and sprinkle with chopped hazelnuts. Serve with a scoop of pear sorbet and decorate with a mint sprig and halved strawberries.

Pannacotta des marais

The combination of salt and sweet flavours works really well in this simple but very effective pudding: the richness will round off a light fish meal to perfection. Serve with a little whipped cream and seasonal fruit.

Preparation: **30 minutes, plus 3 hours cooling**

Cooking: **35 minutes**

Serves: **6**

250g (9oz) caster sugar

600ml (1 pint) milk

2 sachets gelatine (about 11g each)

600ml (1 pint) single cream

pinch of *fleur de sel*

200ml (7fl oz) whipping cream, whipped

6 strawberries, to decorate

sprigs of mint, to decorate

icing sugar, for dusting

Praline biscuits

50g (2oz) chopped almonds

50g (2oz) caster sugar

Place 200g (7oz) of the sugar in a small non-stick pan and gently heat over a medium heat to dissolve until it forms a golden caramel. Remove the pan from the heat.

Warm 200ml (7fl oz) of the milk in another pan, sprinkle in the gelatine and leave on a very low heat to gently dissolve the gelatine.

Place the remaining milk and sugar and the cream in a pan and just bring to the boil. Remove from the heat and stir in the caramel sauce. Pour a little of the milk back into the caramel pan and return to a low heat to dissolve any caramel that has set in the pan. Pour this back into the creamy mixture, adding the salt and dissolved gelatine liquid and mix well.

For the praline biscuits, line a baking sheet with baking parchment. Place the almonds and sugar in a small non-stick pan and place over a low heat, stirring with a metal spoon until the sugar has melted and formed a golden caramel. Quickly pour on to the lined baking sheet and spread evenly. Leave to cool and set.

Pour the creamy mixture into 6 individual serving glasses and chill for 3 hours, or until set. Spoon the whipped cream on top of the cooked creams and decorate each with a strawberry, a mint sprig, two praline biscuits and a dusting of icing sugar.

Aquitaine

Aquitaine is a large area of France with the Atlantic to the west, productive rolling countryside to the north, Poitou-Charentes and Limousin to the east and the mountainous mid Pyrénées and Spain to the south. Bordeaux is the capital of the region, which has become famous for its amazing wines – red and white, sweet dessert and Cognac. Along with an abundance and variety of wines comes some wonderful food. Vast fields of cereals and vegetables and free-range duck farms run alongside the Garonne river, then, travelling further towards Agen, there are prunes and tubby Marmande tomatoes, which are named after their town of origin. Travel inland and charollais cows are readily abundant, grazing in the fields. Back out to the Atlantic coast you'll find a vast array of fish, which are caught and brought into the markets every day. The tidal waterways also make great oyster beds, for which the area is famous. This region of France is the adventurous cook's pantry, supplying everything from field to sea.

New season garlic soup with poilâne toast

Soupe à l'ail et pain poilâne

New season garlic has a beautiful pinky-purple colour with a green stem. The flavour and aroma is so clean and fresh it always reminds me of spring and makes my heart beat with the thought of warm summer days, filling markets with seasonal produce.

Preparation: **15 minutes**

Cooking: **40 minutes**

Serves: **4**

2 new season garlic bulbs

175ml (6fl oz) olive oil

125g (4½oz) bacon, chopped

125g (4½oz) potato, chopped

1.5 litres (2¾ pints) chicken or vegetable stock

bunch of fresh thyme

2 bay leaves

sea salt and freshly ground black pepper

2 slices poilâne sourdough bread, toasted

bunch of fresh parsley, chopped

Crush, peel and chop the garlic and place in a saucepan with a little of the oil and all the bacon and potato. Sauté gently over a low heat for 8 minutes, without browning.

Add the stock, herbs and seasoning, bring to the boil and simmer for 30 minutes. Remove the herbs and add the remaining oil. Blend rapidly with a hand-held electric blender until smooth and emulsified. Check the seasoning and adjust if necessary.

To serve, place half a slice of the toasted bread in each soup bowl, top with chopped parsley and ladle over the soup.

Poached eggs with red wine and shallots

Oeufs pochés au vin rouge

An unusual dish from Burgundy: eggs are poached in red wine and served with shallots, garlic and bacon. Believe me, it is delicious and makes a tasty supper dish or starter.

Preparation: **15 minutes**

Cooking: **20–25 minutes**

Serves: **4**

5 pink shallots, sliced

25g (1oz) butter

1 garlic clove, crushed

3 sprigs of fresh thyme

1 bay leaf

250ml (9fl oz) red wine

1 tbsp balsamic vinegar

4 eggs

4 thick slices ham or back bacon

4 slices sourdough bread, toasted

sea salt and freshly ground black pepper

small bunch of fresh chives, snipped, to garnish

Place the shallots and butter in a pan and gently sauté for 10 minutes until soft but not browned. Add the garlic, thyme and bay leaf and cook for another 5 minutes. Pour in the red wine and vinegar, bring to the boil and simmer until the liquid has reduced by half.

Crack the eggs into 4 small cups. Bring a wide pan of water to a rolling simmer, then turn the heat off. Quickly and carefully slip each of the eggs into the water. Place a lid on the pan and leave the eggs to cook in the still hot water for 6 minutes.

If using bacon, grill on each side for 3 minutes. Place the hot toast on warm serving plates and add the bacon or ham. Remove the eggs from the pan with a draining spoon, allowing excess moisture to run off, and place the eggs on the ham. To serve, top with the red wine and shallot sauce, add a twist of pepper and garnish with chives.

Leek and mustard tart

Tarte aux poireaux et à la moutarde

Every time I see a leek, I just think of French food! Every good kitchen in France uses this vegetable either as part of a recipe, or as its leading ingredient. This wonderful tart is a variation on the classic quiche.

Preparation: **40 minutes, plus 30 minutes resting**

Cooking: **about 1 hour**

Serves: **4**

Pastry

175g (6oz) plain flour, plus extra for dusting

115g (4oz) butter

1 egg, beaten

Filling

1 tbsp olive oil

500g (1lb 2oz) leeks, sliced

2 eggs

2 tbsp Dijon mustard

125ml (4fl oz) single cream

sea salt and freshly ground black pepper

125g (4½oz) brie, thinly sliced

For the pastry, rub the flour and butter together until the mixture resembles breadcrumbs. Add the egg and bind the pastry together, forming a ball. Wrap in cling film and place in the fridge to chill for 30 minutes. Preheat the oven to 180°C/350°F/Gas 4.

Roll the pastry out on a floured surface and use it to line a 20cm (8-inch) tart tin. Prick the base with a fork and line with baking parchment and baking beans. Bake blind in the oven for 20 minutes, then remove the baking parchment and beans and bake for a further 15 minutes.

Meanwhile, prepare the filling. Heat the oil in large pan, add the leeks and sauté on a medium heat for 10 minutes, stirring constantly. Whisk the eggs with the mustard, cream and seasoning.

Place the leeks in the cooked pastry case, pour in the egg mixture and scatter with the sliced brie. Bake for 20 minutes, then turn off the heat and leave the tart in the oven for a further 10 minutes, until the egg mixture is set.

Sea bass with seasoned vegetables

Bar et légumes assaisonnés

Sea bass has such a delicate flavour; this simple method of cooking is ideal for this fine fish. Roseval potatoes, from France, have a vivid carmine skin that contrasts with the yellow, waxy flesh, often with a pink blush. They have a truly superb flavour, but any other small variety of potato could be used if you cannot source them.

Preparation: **10 minutes**

Cooking: **45 minutes**

Serves: **4**

4 tbsp olive oil

1kg (2lb 4oz) Roseval potatoes, or other small variety, cut into wedges

2 garlic bulbs

6 carrots, peeled and cut into lengths

3 leeks, trimmed and cut into lengths

bunch of parsley stalks

1 x 2kg (4½lb) whole sea bass or 2 smaller ones, gutted

1 lemon, sliced

sea salt and freshly ground black pepper

Preheat the oven to 180°C/350°F/Gas 4. Pour the oil into a large roasting pan and toss the potatoes in the oil. Cut the garlic bulbs in half across their width and add to the pan. Place the pan in the oven and cook for 20 minutes. Add the carrots to the potatoes for the last 10 minutes of their cooking time.

Remove the pan from the oven and set aside the garlic bulbs. Add the leeks and parsley stalks to the pan and stir the vegetables to mix.

Place the sea bass on top of the vegetables and stuff the cavity with the garlic cloves and sliced lemon. Season and cover with baking parchment. Bake for 12–15 minutes, then remove the paper and cook for a further 10 minutes, until the fish and potatoes are tender.

Chilli lobster thermidor

Homard thermidor au piment

Sometimes lobsters can be picked up for a song; that's when I get cooking this recipe, although I miss out the chilli for the kids! I like to serve it with a green salad.

Preparation: **30 minutes**

Cooking: **45 minutes**

Serves: **4**

2 live lobsters, about 750g–1kg (1lb 10oz–2lb 4oz) in total

85g (3oz) butter

2 shallots, chopped

1 fresh red chilli, deseeded and diced

1 garlic clove, finely chopped

bunch of fresh parsley, chopped

25g (1oz) flour

100ml (3½fl oz) white wine

1 tsp Dijon mustard

sea salt and freshly ground black pepper

85g (3oz) Parmesan cheese, grated

Heat a pan of water large enough to take both lobsters. When the water is boiling, add the lobsters, cover and cook for 12 minutes. Remove the lobsters and continue to boil, reducing the lobster stock to 300ml (½ pint). Set the stock aside.

When the lobsters are cool enough to handle, cut the heads off and cut the tails in half. Remove the black intestine thread and discard, then remove the meat. Place the empty shells on a baking sheet and slice the lobster meat into 2.5cm (1-inch) pieces.

Heat 50g (2oz) of the butter in a pan, add the shallots, chilli and garlic and sauté for 5 minutes until soft. Add the lobster meat and chopped parsley, turn off the heat and cover to keep warm.

Melt the remaining butter in a separate pan and stir in the flour, making a roux base. Remove the pan from the heat and slowly add the wine and reserved lobster stock, blending to a smooth sauce. Add the mustard and seasoning, return to the heat and gently bring to the boil, stirring all the time. Preheat a hot grill.

Spoon a little of the béchamel sauce into each lobster shell, top with the lobster mixture then spoon over the remaining sauce. Sprinkle with Parmesan and grill until bubbling and golden.

Sautéed squid salad with grapefruit and leaves

Salade de calamars sautés et pamplemousse

Squid is abundant off all of the French coasts and I was inspired to create this lovely salad after eating it in a little café near Biarritz. The grapefruit just cuts through the rich sautéed squid flavours, adding a sweet but sharp twist.

Preparation: **30 minutes**

Cooking: **2 minutes**

Serves: **4**

2 garlic cloves, finely chopped

2 fresh red chillies, seeds left in, finely chopped

bunch of fresh parsley, chopped

3 pink grapefruit

1 tsp caster sugar

sea salt and freshly ground black pepper

125ml (4fl oz) olive oil

1 crunchy head of escarole lettuce

300g (10oz) small squid, cleaned

50g (2oz) flour

Mix the garlic, chillies and parsley together and set aside.

Using a sharp knife, slice the top and base off the grapefruits and then cut away the skin, revealing the pink juicy flesh. Cut the grapefruit between the membranes, making segments without any pith or skin.

Squeeze the juice from the remaining grapefruit core into a bowl, whisk with the caster sugar and seasoning, then slowly drizzle in 100ml (3½fl oz) of the oil while whisking.

Tear the lettuce into leaves, wash and spin dry in a salad spinner. Add the leaves to the grapefruit dressing, toss well to coat, then divide between 4 serving plates. Top the leaves with the prepared grapefruit segments.

Toss the squid in the flour until evenly covered. Heat the remaining oil in a large frying pan and sauté the squid rapidly for 2 minutes. Do not overcook as they will turn tough. Lift and drain the squid into a large bowl, add the garlic, parsley and chilli mixture and toss. Spoon on to the salad and serve at once.

Duck rillettes with green peppercorns

Rillettes de canard au poivre vert

Traditionally this is a dish that is made with the carcass of a bird. This is why I love French cooking; nothing is ever wasted and every part of the animal is used to create its own dish. I have chosen to make this dish with duck legs as it yields more than the traditional one, but do try making it with duck carcasses if you ever have some left over.

Preparation: **15 minutes, plus 1 hour setting**

Cooking: **2½ hours**

Serves: **4**

3 duck legs

300g (10oz) pork belly

200ml (7fl oz) white wine

2 garlic cloves, whole and unpeeled

1 tsp crushed mustard seeds

sea salt and freshly ground black pepper

2 tsp fresh green peppercorns, drained

toasted bread slices, to serve

Preheat the oven to 150°C/300°F/Gas 2. Place the duck and pork in a roasting pan, add the wine, garlic cloves, mustard seeds and seasoning and stir well. Cover with foil and place in the oven to cook for 2½ hours.

Remove the pan from the oven and pour off the fat through a sieve set over a bowl. Place the meat in a separate bowl and set aside until cool enough to handle.

Remove the skin and bones from the duck and shred the meat by hand. Remove the rind and any small bones from the pork and again shred the meat. Mix well in a bowl, add the peppercorns, then place the mixture in a terrine, pressing down with your hands.

Heat the fat again and pass through a piece of muslin to strain. Pour the fat over the meat, making a thin layer on top. Place in the fridge to set for at least 1 hour. It can be stored for up to 1 week. Serve at room temperature with toasted bread.

Pears poached in spiced red wine with chocolate sauce

Poires Richelieu sauce au chocolat

Do not rush this recipe as leaving the pears to steep overnight in the wine intensifies the flavour. The chocolate sauce just adds a level of true French decadence!

Preparation: **10 minutes, plus overnight steeping**

Cooking: **40 minutes**

Serves: **4**

4 medium-ripe pears with stalks

1 bottle red wine (Claret/red Bordeaux is best)

4 cloves

1 star anise

2 cardamom pods

115g (4oz) caster sugar

Chocolate sauce

100ml (3½fl oz) double cream

50g (2oz) butter

115g (4oz) dark chocolate

50g (2oz) caster sugar

Peel the pears carefully, keeping the stalk intact: I find it's best to peel from top to bottom in one movement as it helps to show off their beautiful shape. Place the pears in a saucepan, cover with the wine and add the spices and sugar. Place a sheet of greaseproof paper on top of the pears and a lid that is slightly too small for the pan. (This helps to keep the pears submerged in the wine.) Simmer for 25 minutes, turning occasionally so that they evenly stain in the wine. Leave the pears to steep in the spiced wine overnight.

To make the chocolate sauce, place the cream and butter in a pan and heat gently to melt the butter. Break in the chocolate and add the sugar, then remove the pan from the heat and stir the contents until the chocolate has melted, the sugar has dissolved and the sauce is evenly blended.

Gently reheat the pears for 8 minutes. Serve them with a little of the strained wine juice and pour a spoonful of chocolate sauce over each. Chill the left-over pear stock and freeze to use again.

Goats' cheese and cherry compote

Compote de cerises et fromage de chèvre

I love to buy these beautiful little goats' cheese crottins. At one particular farm that I visited, it was so lovely to select from the fresh, young and mild-flavoured crottins, the slightly older ones (which to me have the best flavour) and the vintage type, which are hard and dry, and rich in flavour. The choice depends on personal taste, but each variety lends itself to a particular method of cooking and any good shop should give you a sample to help you decide your preference.

Preparation: **10 minutes, plus cooling**

Cooking: **15 minutes**

Serves: **4**

300g (10oz) stoned cherries

2 tbsp water

4 fresh young goats' cheeses

Place the cherries in a non-stick pan with the water. Cover and gently warm over a low heat for 15 minutes, adding a little more water if needed. Remove from the heat and cool.

Place a goats' cheese on each serving plate and spoon over the cherry compote. Serve immediately.

La Tupina
6 rue Porte de la Monnaie
33800 Bordeaux

Tel +33 (0)5 56 91 56 37

www.latupina.com

Owner: Jean Pierre Xiradakis

Chef: Bruno Manusset

*Open daily 12noon – 2pm
and 7 – 11pm*

La Tupina

This old quarter of Bordeaux was traditionally the money printers' area. Jean Pierre Xiradakis grew up here, helping in his family's hardware shop and watching his grandmother cook. Today this part of Bordeaux is the 'Bobo' area, meaning bourgeois and bohemian; La Tupina has done a great deal to add to this scene. Wander your way around the cobbled streets and you will enter this famed and traditional bistro, which opened in 1968, and which has a larger-than-life fireplace with a wooden table in front crammed with fresh local produce. Jean Pierre Xiradakis has created a lovely home-from-home feel that is truly authentic. There are many different rooms all crammed with artifacts and tables with checkered cloths, and as soon as you sit down and start to absorb the atmosphere, a smiling waiter brings a plate of crudités: sliced salami and small pieces of chitterlings sautéed in garlic and parsley, and a large basket of bread and Beurre Echiré, which is a favourite with good chefs. Already you know that this is going to be a feast to remember.

La tupina means 'cooking pot' and many of the dishes are cooked in a pot, over the large and roaring fire. One imagines that granny should be cooking at this fire, but no, instead a good-looking young man is making light work of the spit roast, potatoes cooked in goose fat and duck breast with morel mushrooms. The food is simple but delicious as the raw produce is selected with great care and attention; the menu informs you that the black pig comes from the Pyrénées and the duck from Landes. This is traditional south-western fare at its best. Arrive here hungry and you will leave well stocked. The wine list is endless and, as a special touch, regular guests have been given their own wine lockers downstairs in the cave to store speciality wines that are gifts from Jean Pierre, or which need to be purchased while available for the next meal when they return!

Wild mushrooms with parsley

Cèpes à la persillade

Bruno, the chef at La Tupina, says that pepper is not a friend of the wild mushroom, so use it sparingly! This dish is delicious served either on its own or as an accompaniment to plain grilled meat, such as the Spatchcock wood pigeon opposite. This simple method of cooking suits as all the effort will have gone into gathering the mushrooms from the forest.

Preparation: **10 minutes**

Cooking: **8 minutes**

Serves: **4**

750g (1lb 10oz) mixed wild mushrooms

1 tbsp duck fat

2 garlic cloves, finely chopped

bunch of fresh parsley, finely chopped

sea salt and freshly ground black pepper

Trim the base off the mushrooms and clean with a brush or cloth. Cut the large mushrooms thickly and leave small ones whole.

Heat the duck fat in a large frying pan, add the larger mushrooms first and cook for 3 minutes, then add the smaller ones and cook for a further 3 minutes, tossing carefully. Remove and place on kitchen paper to remove any excess duck fat.

Return the mushrooms to the pan, sprinkle in the garlic, parsley and seasoning, toss well and serve.

Spatchcock wood pigeon

Palombes en crapaudine

Jean Pierre Xiradakis says: 'If the weather is fine, fire up the barbecue and cook over hot coals.' This method of cooking also works well for quails and chickens — try basting the chickens with a mixture of vinegar, olive oil, chopped shallots and garlic. **Crapaudine** *means 'toad' in French and once the bird is cut and prepared, its shape resembles that of a large toad, hence the unusual name!*

Preparation: **25 minutes**

Cooking: **12–20 minutes**

Serves: **4**

4 wood pigeons, cleaned

50g (2oz) lard or 4 tbsp olive oil, if preferred

sea salt and freshly ground black pepper

To prepare the pigeons, place each on its breast and cut down one side of the backbone from one end to the other (do not cut through the breast), making it possible to butterfly and lay the bird out flat. Cut down the other side of the backbone and discard, then with the flat of your hand press on to the bird flattening it entirely.

Preheat a hot grill or prepare the barbecue coals. Rub the pigeons all over with the lard or oil and seasoning. Cook for 6–8 minutes on each side if you like the flesh pink, 8 minutes for medium and 10 minutes for well done.

Pork and haricot bean stew

Cassoulet

Preparation: **15 minutes,
plus soaking the beans
the day before**

Cooking: **45 minutes
(for the beans), then 1 hour**

Serves: **6**

**500g (1lb 2oz) haricot beans
(lingot variety recommended)**

2 onions

1 clove

1 carrot, chopped

5 garlic cloves

**1 bouquet garni (parsley, bay,
rosemary, thyme)**

115g (4oz) pork rind

**250g (9oz) salt pork belly,
chopped**

50g (2oz) duck fat

**300g (10oz) shoulder of lamb,
cubed**

**300g (10oz) loin of pork,
cubed**

1 dsp tomato purée

**500g (1lb 2oz) *confit de canard*
(preserved duck),
cut into portions**

**300g (10oz) Toulouse
sausages, thickly sliced**

**sea salt and freshly ground
black pepper**

**300g (10oz) fresh
breadcrumbs**

*This famous dish from the south-west of France varies
from bistro to bistro, with everyone declaring theirs to
be authentic! This recipe is delicious and, once you have
gathered all the ingredients, it's so easy to make. This is
a truly magnificent and memorable meal for a celebration,
with something in the pot for everyone!*

The day before, soak the beans in cold water, changing the water
2–3 times. The next day, place 2.5 litres (4½ pints) fresh water in a
large pan with the soaked beans, 1 onion studded with the clove, the
chopped carrot, 2 cloves garlic, bouquet garni, pork rind and chopped
salt pork belly. Place a lid on, just bring to the boil, then reduce the
heat and simmer for 45 minutes, removing the froth that rises during
cooking. When cooked, remove the bouquet garni and pork rind and
discard. Drain the bean mixture and reserve the cooking liquor.

Heat the duck fat in a large, flameproof casserole dish, add the lamb
and pork and fry until browned. Chop the remaining onion and
cloves of garlic, add to the meat pan and cook for 2 minutes, then
add the tomato purée and 1 litre (1¾ pints) of the reserved cooking
liquor from the bean mixture. Bring to the boil, then reduce the
heat, cover and simmer for 20 minutes. Meanwhile, preheat the
oven to 180°C/350°F/Gas 4.

Remove the excess fat from the preserved duck and add the duck
to the cassoulet with the sausages and seasoning and bring to a
simmer for 5 minutes. Remove from the heat and add the beans in
a layer on top of the cooked meats – the juice should just come to
the top of the beans – top up if needed with a little extra from the
reserved cooking liquor.

Finally, top with a layer of breadcrumbs and place in the oven to
bake for 15 minutes. Reduce the oven temperature to 160°C/325°F/
Gas 3 and cook for a further 20 minutes, until golden and bubbling.

VILLARD-RECULAS

VILLARD-RECULAS

Construction
de la
"Bergerie"
en
1970
~

Rhône-Alpes

Lyon is the second-largest city in France. It is famed for its cuisine and is the gateway to the south. It is also home to the large wine regions of the Côtes du Rhône and Beaujolais. The city of Lyon boasts more bistros, cafés and restaurants per head than anywhere in the world; on every corner you come across an eating house. Traditionally, these were called *bouchons* and were places that offered a glass of wine and typical traditional Lyonnais food – meat, offal, duck and sausages. There are still many all over Lyon and, although only a few belong to Les Authentiques Bouchons Lyonnais, many of the others are also good.

Then travelling east, you climb into the Alps, which are also rich in their own Savoie wines, tasty dense cheeses, goats' cheese, cured hams, an abundance of saucissons and, in the summer, small alpine strawberries and myrtles, potatoes and the ringing bells of cows and sheep wandering the meadows. In the summer, the mountains are a hive of activity as the soil is rich and every possible inch is levelled to grow fruit and vegetables. This produce is then prepared and stored ready for the colder winter months, when it is not always so easy to get good-quality produce – some of the villages are far away from large towns and may even be cut off by the snow, so the villagers must ensure that they have enough food for the winter season. It is a hard life but the locals really understand the weather and know how to take advantage of the warm summer months and grow as much produce as they can. There is a long winter ski season here, but most tourists who come do not get a true impression of what it's like to live in the mountains year round. It's a very special and peaceful place to be, especially when you are 'snugged-up' with some good mountain food and wine!

Cheesy potato gratin

Tartiflette

*All across the Alps variations of **Tartiflette** are served with the additions of local mountain hams, lardons, local cheeses or mushrooms from the forests.*

Preparation: **30 minutes**

Cooking: **45 minutes**

Serves: **4**

1.5kg (3lb 5oz) potatoes, peeled

1 tbsp olive oil

1 onion, sliced

200g (7oz) smoked streaky bacon, chopped

sprig of fresh thyme

100ml (3½fl oz) white wine

sea salt and freshly ground black pepper

1 garlic clove, crushed

1 x 500g Reblochon cheese

Preheat the oven to 180°C/350°F/Gas 4. Cook the potatoes in a large pan of boiling water for 15 minutes, until just soft. Drain and, when cool enough to handle, slice.

Heat the olive oil and add the onion and bacon and cook until just golden. Add the thyme, wine and seasoning, simmer for 5 minutes, then remove the thyme sprig.

Rub the inside of an ovenproof dish with the crushed garlic, layer in half the potatoes, top with the bacon mixture and follow with the remaining potatoes, making another layer.

Place the whole piece of cheese in the centre of the dish on top of the potatoes. Cook in the oven for 25 minutes until golden.

King's Beaufort soufflé

Soufflé du roi Beaufort

Many bistros serve fantastic soufflés, bursting and rising out of their pots, using a variety of strong-tasting, local cheeses. However, I call this recipe 'the King's soufflé' because, of all the hard mountain cheeses, Beaufort is, quite simply, the best. It has a rich, dense, fruity and lightly nutty flavour, which makes a beautifully tasty soufflé. Serve with a crisp green salad.

Preparation: **20 minutes**

Cooking: **30 minutes**

Serves: **4, as starter**

50g (2oz) butter, plus extra for greasing

40g (1½oz) flour

200ml (7fl oz) milk

sea salt and freshly ground black pepper

½ tsp Dijon mustard

5 eggs, separated

100g (3½oz) Beaufort cheese, finely grated

Preheat the oven to 200°C/400°F/Gas 6. Using a little extra butter, rub the inside of 4 medium-sized individual soufflé dishes. Melt the butter in a pan, then remove from the heat, add the flour and mix to a smooth roux. Return the pan to a low heat and cook for 30 seconds. Slowly pour in the milk and bring to the boil, stirring constantly to make a smooth sauce.

Remove the pan from the heat, add seasoning and mustard to the sauce, then beat in the egg yolks and the grated cheese, reserving a little to sprinkle on the top. Stir and leave in a warm place.

Whisk the egg whites until stiff in a large bowl, add the cheese sauce and fold in as quickly as possible. Spoon the mixture into the prepared soufflé dishes – they should be about two-thirds full. Quickly place them in the oven and bake for 15 minutes.

Sprinkle the soufflés with the reserved cheese and then reduce the oven to 190°C/375°F/Gas 5 and cook them for a further 5–8 minutes until they are puffed and golden. Serve immediately, straight from the oven to the table, and enjoy!

Calf's liver, bacon and Aligot potatoes

Foie de veau à l'Anglaise et pommes Aligot

In the central Auvergne region of France, where Cantal cheese is produced, Aligot potatoes are a staple. Cantal is a young, hard cheese with a simple flavour but, when married with the potatoes and beaten like billy-o, it delivers this heavenly, wicked dish. The French often serve the potatoes with scissors to cut the super-elastic potato mix – otherwise it's a long stretch!

Preparation: **20 minutes**

Cooking: **40 minutes**

Serves: **4**

8 smoked back bacon rashers

1 tbsp olive oil

20g (scant 1oz) butter

4 x 150g (5oz) thin slices calf's liver

200ml (7fl oz) red Burgundy

Aligot potatoes

800g (1lb 12oz) floury potatoes, peeled

50g (2oz) butter

4 tbsp single cream

2 garlic cloves, crushed

300g (10oz) Cantal cheese, grated

sea salt and freshly ground black pepper

For the Aligot potatoes, simmer the potatoes for 20 minutes until soft, drain, then return to the pan and toss over a low heat to evaporate any excess moisture. Pass the potatoes through a sieve – this is important as it helps get that magical consistency.

Warm the butter, cream and crushed garlic in a large pan, add the potatoes, grated cheese and seasoning and then beat rapidly over a very low heat until you have a smooth creamy consistency. Cover and keep warm.

Grill the bacon until golden and crispy. Heat the oil and butter in a frying pan and, when melted, cook the liver for just 2 minutes on each side. Remove from the pan and keep warm.

Add the wine to the pan and simmer rapidly to reduce by half. Serve the liver, bacon and Aligot potatoes together and spoon over a little sauce.

Roast quail and grapes from the vine

Cailles rôties aux raisins

In the autumn, when these birds are at their best, you will see them on many menus. Traditionally they are game birds, but often they are farmed due to the high demand for them. Served with grapes plucked fresh from the vine, this makes a beautifully easy but tasty dish.

Preparation: **15 minutes**

Cooking: **25 minutes**

Serves: **4**

4 quail

4 bay leaves

bunch of fresh thyme

4 streaky bacon rashers

1 tbsp olive oil

sea salt and freshly ground black pepper

200ml (7fl oz) white wine

200g (7oz) mixed seedless grapes

Preheat the oven to 190°C/375°F/Gas 5. Stuff each quail with a bay leaf and small sprig of thyme and wrap in a rasher of bacon. Rub with the oil and seasoning, place in a small roasting tin and roast for 20 minutes, or until cooked through.

Remove the quail from the oven, place in another cooking pan and keep warm. Place the roasting tin directly on the stove top, add the white wine to the juices and boil rapidly for 4 minutes to reduce. Add the grapes and seasoning, stir, then serve the quail with the grape sauce spooned over.

Sauerkraut with ham and sausages

Choucroute à l'Alsacienne

In the past sauerkraut was made in large quantities in a wooden barrel and used as a staple vegetable throughout the winter months. It is very simple to make: it consists of finely sliced cabbage and salt packed into a wooden barrel and covered with a tightly fitting lid with a weight placed on top, which is left to ferment for a minimum of three weeks. Any excess liquid is then drained off from the top and the sauerkraut is stirred. (This process is repeated every time some is used.) In the recipe below I suggest that you buy ready-made sauerkraut, as only a small amount is required. The chef of the bistro where I ate this dish told me that he uses 30–40 heads of white cabbage to make one batch!

Preparation: **15 minutes, plus 30 minutes soaking**

Cooking: **1½ hours**

Serves: **4**

700g (1lb 9oz) salt pork belly, cut into 4 slices

1 tbsp goose fat

1kg (2lb 4oz) prepared sauerkraut

freshly ground black pepper

3 juniper berries, ground

4 plump pork sausages

100ml (3½fl oz) white wine

750ml–1 litre (about 1½ pints) pork or chicken stock

1kg (2lb 4oz) potatoes, peeled

bunch of fennel leaves, chopped

Soak the salt pork belly in cold water for 30 minutes to rinse off any excess salt. Preheat the oven to 180°C/350°F/Gas 4.

Melt the goose fat in a large casserole pot and add half the sauerkraut. Season with pepper and ground juniper berries, add the salt pork belly and sausages and spoon the remaining sauerkraut over the top. Add the wine and just cover with stock. Place a lid on top and cook in the oven for 1 hour.

Cut the potatoes into even-sized pieces, add to the pot and cook for a further 30 minutes. Stir in the chopped fennel leaves. Serve the sauerkraut and potatoes topped with the pork and sausage.

Sticky pork ribs with wine and garlic marinade

Côtes de porc marinées au vin et à l'ail

When on a skiing holiday many years ago, my family and I visited a particularly good mountain bistro. The sticky pork ribs that were served there were so tasty that I had to ask for the recipe so that I could make it back at home. Here it is!

Preparation: **15 minutes, plus overnight marinating**

Cooking: **1 hour**

Serves: **4**

5 garlic cloves, crushed

2cm (¾-inch) piece fresh root ginger, minced

1 red onion, diced

200ml (7fl oz) red wine

2 tbsp honey

2 tbsp soy sauce

1 tbsp tomato purée

1 tbsp sugar

salt and freshly ground black pepper

1 tbsp vegetable oil

1.5–2kg (3½–4½lb) pork ribs

Place the garlic, ginger, onion and wine in a blender and whizz until smooth. Add the honey, soy sauce, purée, sugar and seasoning and whizz again. Smear the mixture all over the ribs, cover and leave in the fridge overnight.

Preheat the oven to 160°C/325°F/Gas 3. Lightly oil a roasting tin, add the ribs in a single layer and place in the oven to roast for 30 minutes. Turn and roast for another 30 minutes, or until cooked through. To serve, eat with your fingers and make sure you have big napkins at the table!

Roasted bone marrow

Os à moelle rôti

Preparation: **10 minutes**

Cooking: **45 minutes**

Serves: **4**

12 slices shin of beef or thigh bones of beef

bunch of fresh parsley, chopped

slices of toast, to serve

Bone marrow is served all over Lyon as a starter, either boiled or roasted. I prefer the roasting method as it intensifies the very delicate flavour. Bone marrow is also used to enrich **pot au feu***: it is simmered with the meat and then scooped out and the bones discarded. The resourceful cook, however, will use it again in a stockpot!*

Preheat the oven to 160°C/325°F/Gas 3. Place the bones in a roasting tin, flat side up, and place in the oven to roast for 45 minutes.

Serve 3 bones per person and sprinkle with chopped parsley. Serve with hot toast and a teaspoon for scooping out the marrow.

Croque monsieur with mustard

Croque monsieur à la moutarde

Preparation: **5 minutes**

Cooking: **10 minutes**

Serves: **2**

4 slices sourdough bread

knob of butter

Dijon mustard (optional)

2 slices cured ham

100g (3½oz) Gruyère cheese, thinly sliced

bunch of watercress

Another quick lunchtime snack that can be found in local bistros and is really delicious if made with market-fresh quality ingredients. Turn this into a croque-madam by topping with a poached egg.

Preheat the grill to medium. Butter each slice of bread on one side and spread with mustard, if liked. Cover 2 slices with the ham and then top with the sliced cheese. Top with the remaining bread, buttered side down.

Place under the grill and cook on each side until the toast is golden. Remove, cut in half and serve garnished with watercress.

Walnut and caramel tart

Tarte aux noix et au caramel

Grenoble is famous for its walnuts and they are used in many recipes. This one is particularly wicked and appears on many menus. Serve with rich, dark coffee.

Preparation: **30 minutes, plus 1 hour resting the pastry and 1 hour setting the tart**

Cooking: **40 minutes**

Serves: **4–6**

Pastry

150g (5oz) plain flour

75g (2½oz) cold butter, cut into small pieces

25g (1oz) caster sugar

1 large egg, whisked

Filling

75g (2½oz) caster sugar

40g (1½oz) butter

150ml (¼ pint) double cream

175g (6oz) shelled walnuts

First make the pastry. Place the flour and butter in a bowl and rub together quickly with your fingers until it resembles breadcrumbs. Add the sugar and mix through. Mix the whisked egg into the pastry mix using a flat-bladed knife, bringing the pastry together to form a dough ball. Wrap in cling film and chill in the fridge for 1 hour.

Preheat the oven to 190°C/375°F/Gas 5. Place the pastry on a cold work surface, press out with the heel of your hand, then roll out to fit and line a 23cm (9-inch) loose-based flan tin. Do not stretch the pastry to fit. Trim away the excess pastry from around the edge of the tin. Prick the base with a fork. Line with baking parchment, fill with baking beans and cook for 20 minutes. Reduce the oven temperature to 160°C/325°F/Gas 3, remove the beans and baking parchment and return the pastry case to the oven to bake for a further 15 minutes.

For the filling, place the sugar in a thick-based, non-stick pan and heat until dissolved and turned to caramel. Remove from the heat and leave to cool for 5 minutes, add the butter and cream, then return to the heat and stir until smooth and blended.

Scatter the walnuts in the cooked pastry case, pour over the caramel and leave to set for at least 1 hour.

Mountain fruit streusel

Streusel aux fruits de la montagne

In the summer the mountains are covered with myrtles. They are painstaking to pick but, in the sunny fresh air, who cares! This dish was served at a beautiful little bistro where there was no menu; you just ate what came from the kitchen. Here is my interpretation of what was a heavenly use of all those myrtles.

Preparation: **20 minutes**

Cooking: **40 minutes**

Serves: **4**

100g (3½oz) butter

100g (3½oz) caster sugar

25g (1oz) hazelnuts, chopped

25g (1oz) almonds, chopped

85g (3oz) plain flour

750g (1lb 10oz) apples

500g (1lb 2oz) myrtles or blueberries

2 tbsp runny honey

1 tsp ground cinnamon

Preheat the oven to 180°C/350°F/Gas 4. Blend together the butter and sugar, add the nuts and flour and stir through to make a crumble mixture.

Peel, core and slice the apples and place in an ovenproof dish, along with the myrtles. Sprinkle over the nut topping evenly, drizzle with honey and sift over the cinnamon. Place in the oven and bake for 40 minutes.

Pancakes with myrtles and fromage blanc

Crêpes aux myrtilles et fromage blanc

With the abundance of myrtle berries there exist many different recipes that use them. This one is a firm favourite with children, and can be found in many bistros and is easily repeated at home.

Preparation: **5 minutes, plus 30 minutes resting**

Cooking: **about 20 minutes**

Serves: **4 (makes 8 pancakes)**

100g (3½oz) plain flour
1 large egg
300ml (½ pint) milk
butter, for cooking pancakes
8 tbsp fromage blanc (soft curd cheese)
400g (14oz) myrtles
50g (2oz) caster sugar

Place the flour in a bowl, whisk the egg and milk together and slowly mix into the flour, whisking to make a smooth batter. Cover and leave to rest for 30 minutes.

Heat a medium-sized frying pan, brush with a little melted butter, then add a ladleful of batter and tilt the pan to spread it thinly and evenly. Cook for 1–2 minutes, flip with the help of a spatula and cook for a further 1 minute, then transfer to a warm plate. Repeat until all the batter is used.

To serve, place a pancake on each serving plate, add a spoonful of fromage blanc and a few myrtles and sprinkle with sugar.

La Bergerie
Le Cloudit
38114 Villard Reculas

Tel +33 (0)4 76 80 36 83

Owners/chefs: François Barlerin &
Laurence Borjon

*Open Winter 20 December – 20 April
9am – 5.30pm*

*Summer 1st weekend July – last weekend
August 10am – 9pm*

La Bergerie

Wind your way up the mountain from the valley below and, in the summer, you will arrive at the door of this pretty-as-a-picture Alpine eatery that sits at 1600m (5249ft). It was built in 1974 but looks far older. In the winter you will need skis, snow-shoes or a skidoo for access, but in the summer you can drive to the door or get there walking, via the meadow. La Bergerie is a family affair; François and Laurence (husband and wife) and François's mother all work hard to serve you a meal in this amazing location. With views of huge mountains all around you, this place is perched up high on the side of the mountain and nestled in a little fold. Everyone who eats here is amazed at the enormity of the view. In the summer you can eat on the balcony surrounded by the grassy meadows and grazing sheep that have been brought up from the south of France to enjoy the rich grass and cooler air. In the winter there is a pretty dining room adorned with Alpine antiques and a warming log fire.

The summer and winter menus here are totally different due to the remote location and the enthusiastic skiers' demand for simple fast food. In the summer it is a destination for long, slow eating and the menu reflects this in being more complex. What makes this place even more unusual is that the chef varies according to the season. On the winter watch, François charges across the piste on his skidoo to deliver produce to the door of La Bergerie and take charge in the kitchen while, in the summer, Laurence produces a more complex menu of Alpine food from the kitchen. François worked around the Alps in various restaurants before returning to this family-run eatery and Laurence learned to cook with her grandmother and enjoys using the skills she gained in her own summer kitchen.

All the recipes here, bar the Pear cake, are from La Bergerie's summer menu.

Villaraise fondue

Fondue Villaraise

Tuck into a bowl of this bubbling, delicious blend of melted mountain cheeses steeped in white wine and a great selection of mountain-cured meats. Great served with a local white wine such as Apremont or Roussette.

Preparation: **25 minutes**
Cooking: **about 10 minutes**
Serves: **6**

300g (10oz) Beaufort cheese
200g (7oz) Comté cheese
300g (10oz) Emmental cheese
400ml (14fl oz) Savoie white wine (such as Apremont)
2 white garlic cloves, crushed
50ml (2fl oz) kirsch
salt and freshly ground black pepper
1 large French bread
16 slices Grisons meat (air-cured), thinly sliced
crisp green salad, to serve

Preheat the oven to 190°C/375°F/Gas 5. Cut the cheeses into approximate 1cm (½-inch) pieces. Pour the wine into a fondue pan or other thick-based, flameproof pan. Add the garlic and bring to the boil.

Reduce the heat to a simmer, add the cheese and stir continuously, using a wooden spoon in a figure-of-eight motion, for about 8 minutes until the mixture is smooth and blended. Stir in the kirsch and seasoning to taste.

Cut the bread into 3cm (1¼-inch) cubes and place on a tray in the oven to bake lightly for 3 minutes. Serve the fondue on a stand with a burner underneath to keep the fondue warm. Serve with a platter of Grisons meat and accompanied by a crisp green salad.

Creamy layered potato bake

Gratin Dauphinois

A perfect gratin is when the cream and milk become rich and thick like paint. François cooks it until the sauce around the potatoes would be good for a 'painter', he tells me laughing! This makes a generous amount but it is real comfort food that just demands seconds.

Preparation: **25 minutes**

Cooking: **1½ hours**

Serves: **6**

2.5kg (5½lb) white floury potatoes, peeled

175g (6oz) butter

3 garlic cloves

salt and freshly ground black pepper

200ml (7fl oz) single cream

approximately 800ml (1 pint 8fl oz) milk

Preheat the oven to 240°C/475°F/Gas 9. Wash the potatoes in water to remove any excess starch, then shake dry. Slice into 4mm (⅛-inch) wafer-thin rounds – a mandolin is best if you have one, or you could use the slicer attachment on a food processor.

Rub a 3-litre (5½-pint) shallow-sided earthenware dish with half the butter. Spread one third of the potatoes and one third of the crushed garlic over the bottom of the dish, then season. Repeat to give two more layers. Top with the remaining butter, then season just with salt.

Pour over the cream and then the milk, to just cover the potatoes (the amount of milk required varies according to the dimensions of the dish).

Place in the oven for 15 minutes, then reduce the temperature to 180°C/350°F/Gas 4 and cook for a further 1¼ hours.

Laurence's pear cake

Le gâteau aux poires de Laurence

This is a family recipe from Laurence's mother. It's for a celebratory cake that was baked when she was a young girl for many birthdays. Now it is very popular with famished skiers!

Preparation: **30 minutes**

Cooking: **55 minutes**

Serves: **6**

375g (13oz) self-raising flour

200g (7oz) caster sugar

125ml (4fl oz) milk

150g (5oz) unsalted butter, melted

4 large eggs

2 tsp baking powder

4 drops pure vanilla extract

2 dsp Poire William liqueur

450g (1lb) canned pear halves (drained weight)

Topping

115g (4oz) unsalted butter, plus extra for buttering the cake tin

75g (2½oz) caster sugar

1 egg yolk

Preheat the oven to 180°C/350°F/Gas 4. Butter the inside of a 23cm (9-inch) non-stick springform cake tin.

Place the flour, sugar, milk, butter, eggs, baking powder, vanilla extract and liqueur in a bowl and mix quickly together until smooth. Transfer the mixture to the buttered cake tin and arrange the pears flat side down over the top of the cake. Bake for 30 minutes.

For the topping, mix together the butter, sugar and egg yolk. Quickly pour over the top of the cake, without removing it from the oven, and cook for a further 25 minutes. Test that it is cooked by inserting a knife – the blade should come out clean. Serve warm or at room temperature.

Brasserie des Brotteaux
1 place Jules Ferry
69006 Lyon

Tel: +33 (0)4 72 74 03 98

www.brasseriedesbrotteaux.com

e.faucon@brasseriedesbrotteaux.com

Owner: Emmanuel Fauçon

Chef: Laurent Morel

*Open 7.30am Continental breakfast,
Lunch 12noon – 4pm*

*Dinner 7.30 – 10.30pm, closing
at midnight*

Closed Sunday

Brasserie des Brotteaux

This is a beautiful brasserie with fantastic traditional glass and ironwork outside and two walls of huge glass windows. Emmanuel Fauçon bought what was then a scruffy and run-down eatery at the young age of 25, despite the fact that his family thought he was mad. Well, some 15 years later, this place has become an elegant and busy brasserie. In the morning the brasserie serves coffee and cake, and at lunchtime it is transformed, with crisp white linen and paper tablecloths, sparkling glasses and a chalked-up 'dish of the day' board in addition to the set menu. While sitting and looking around, you will notice classic, floral French wall tiles that are made by Gilardon, who worked with the popular Art Nouveau architect, Hector Guimard. The floor is also laid with beautiful, blue-patterned tiles. This place oozes French elegance done with ease.

The menu reads very beautifully to match the place, but when your plate arrives the food is simply presented with the most delicious sauces, packed with depth and flavour. The chef, Laurent Morel, used to work at Fernand Point in Vienne, which had two Michelin stars, but then joined Brasserie des Brotteaux and has been here for six years. The theory behind the cooking here is quality and simplicity to deliver a perfectly balanced meal. It must be good because fashion designers John Galliano and Christian Lacroix both eat here and say it's so good, it's like their home dining room! One very refreshing thing is that Emmanuel has a global selection of wines on his list as he says it's important to supply the best. But do not worry, there are also plenty of excellent wines from the Côtes du Rhône!

Creamy mushroom cups with foie gras

Cappuccino de cèpes et foie gras

This is a house speciality that is so popular that it cannot be removed from the menu! It rings of the 1990s, and the mushroom-infused cream makes a heady marriage with the foie gras.

Preparation: **10 minutes**
Cooking: **55 minutes**
Serves: **4**

150g (5oz) foie gras, sliced
25g (1oz) butter
1 shallot, chopped
250g (9oz) ceps or porcini, thinly sliced
100ml (3½fl oz) dry white wine
250ml (9fl oz) veal or chicken stock
400ml (14fl oz) double cream
100ml (3½fl oz) whipping cream, whipped
sea salt and freshly ground black pepper

Sauté the foie gras in half the butter for 1 minute on each side. Remove and set aside to rest.

Sauté the shallot in the remaining butter without colouring. Add the ceps or porcini and gently sauté for a further 10 minutes over a low heat.

Add the white wine and deglaze the pan, reducing the liquid to half over a low heat. Add the stock and again reduce the liquid to half.

Add the double cream, stir and simmer for 20 minutes, then remove from the heat and strain the cream through a fine sieve.

Cut the foie gras into cubes and divide between 4 cappuccino cups or small soup bowls. Pour over the hot strained sauce. Serve topped with whipped cream and sprinkled with seasoning.

Steak with Saint-Marcellin sauce

Demi-poire de boeuf sauce Saint-Marcellin

The sauce for these steaks is made from little melted cheeses, which are named after the town they are from in the Dauphiné region. Due to their creaminess they make an excellent and easy sauce for a quickly cooked steak. Steaks are a staple across France and are cooked with their own regional sauces or traditions, making no two alike! The French have a much broader range of cuts for steaks than elsewhere and, perhaps surprisingly, they often use topside.

Preparation: **10 minutes**

Cooking: **10–15 minutes**

Serves: **2**

10g (scant ½oz) butter

1 small onion, finely chopped

2 shallots, finely chopped

100ml (3½fl oz) red Mâcon wine

100ml (3½fl oz) stock

100ml (3½fl oz) single cream

1 x 80g Saint-Marcellin cheese, chopped

sea salt and freshly ground black pepper

1 tbsp olive oil

2 thinly sliced steaks of choice, such as rump or sirloin

Heat the butter in a pan and sauté the onion and shallots without colouring. Add the wine and simmer until it has evaporated. Add the stock and again simmer until almost evaporated. Stir in the cream and bring to the boil, add the cheese and simmer gently, stirring in until melted. Season to taste and set aside.

Heat the oil in a frying pan and sauté the steak to your liking. Allow 2 minutes each side for rare, 3 minutes for medium and 4–5 minutes for well done. Leave to rest for 5 minutes in a warm place before serving.

Emulsify the sauce with a hand-held blender to lighten and give a mousse-like consistency. Reheat gently. Serve the steaks with the warmed sauce spooned over the top.

Praline tart

Tarte aux pralines

Praline is a sweet made with almonds, hazelnuts and sugar; the roasted nuts are coated with caramel and then ground to a grainy mix. In Lyon they are coloured pink with a little red food colouring, which I have included here as optional.

Preparation: **1 hour, plus 1 hour 20 minutes for chilling the pastry**
Cooking: **1 hour 5 minutes**
Serves: **6–8**

Praline (makes 500g/1lb 2oz)
100g (3½oz) blanched almonds
150g (5oz) blanched hazelnuts
250g (9oz) caster sugar
1 tbsp water
few drops pure vanilla extract
few drops red food colouring (optional)

Pastry
125g (4½oz) butter, softened
125g (4½oz) caster sugar
250g (9oz) plain flour
1 tsp baking powder
1 egg

Filling
400ml (14fl oz) single cream
4 medium eggs, beaten

For the praline, place the nuts in a saucepan and cook over a medium heat, stirring frequently, until golden. In another saucepan, heat the sugar with the water until the sugar dissolves and becomes a golden caramel. Do not stir, just swirl the pan clockwise to evenly dissolve the sugar and stop it catching on the bottom of the pan.

Add the golden nuts to the caramel, mix well, then add the vanilla extract. Pour the praline out on to a baking sheet lined with baking parchment and spread evenly. Leave to cool. Break up and whizz in a blender or food processor until its texture resembles that of coarse sand, and add a few drops of red food colouring, if liked.

For the pastry, rub the butter, sugar, flour and baking powder together in a mixing bowl until the mixture resembles breadcrumbs. Add the egg and mix well with your hands. The pastry should not be sticky; if it is, dust with more flour. Place in the fridge to chill for 1 hour.

Preheat the oven to 180°C/350°F/Gas 4. Roll out the pastry on a lightly floured surface and use to line a 23cm (9-inch) loose-based flan tin. Place in the fridge to rest for 20 minutes, then prick the base with a fork and line with baking parchment and baking beans. Bake blind for 15 minutes. Remove the beans and baking parchment and cook for a further 10 minutes.

Heat the cream and praline in a medium saucepan, slowly reducing over a low heat for 10 minutes, stirring frequently. Remove from the heat, pour into a bowl and leave to cool for 20 minutes in the fridge. Add the beaten eggs, a little at a time, and blend until smooth.

Pour the praline mixture into the pastry case, smooth over the top and bake for 30 minutes until set.

Languedoc

This large and varied region of southern France stretches along the south-west coast and is steeped in history: from the Roman town of Nîmes, which has its own original arena to host bull fights, to Carcassonne, which has two separate towns, the fortified Cité de Carcassonne and the more expansive lower city, the *ville basse*, due to the wars that were fought against the Cathars. The food of this large region is rich and varied, with oysters from the salt lagoons, squid and sardines caught from the Mediterranean, and cherries, apricots and peaches. Again, there is an abundance of vines, which, as is the case in Provence, were planted to provide French soldiers with their quota of a litre of wine a day. Further inland you will find rich plateaux growing a combination of the largest, sweetest peaches I have ever eaten, an abundance of melons and various salad items.

Yet, in the hills and to the west, it is dry and arid – here only sheep can scratch together enough nourishment to survive. This western region, in the foothills of the Pyrénées, is where the famed Roquefort cheese comes from; the story goes that a shepherd boy left his lunch of bread and cheese in a cave for some time and, when he returned, he discovered that it was full of blue veins and had a distinctive, strong but delicious taste. Further north-west is where the famous dish cassoulet comes from and every village serves its own version and claims to have the original recipe!

Pork loin with rhubarb and balsamic vinegar

Filet de porc à la rhubarbe et vinaigre balsamique

An unusual combination, you may think, but the acidity of the rhubarb cuts through the richness of the pork and makes this a beautiful dish.

Preparation: **10 minutes**
Cooking: **40–45 minutes**
Serves: **4**

1 tbsp olive oil
25g (1oz) butter
600g (1lb 5oz) pork loin
200g (7oz) rhubarb
100ml (3½fl oz) chicken stock
50g (2oz) sugar
1 tsp mustard
1 tbsp white wine vinegar
sea salt and freshly ground black pepper

Preheat the oven to 190°C/375°F/Gas 5. Heat the oil and butter in an ovenproof pan and, when foaming, add the pork and brown on all sides. Place in the oven and roast for 25 minutes.

Meanwhile, trim the ends of the rhubarb and cut the stems on a diagonal into 4cm (1½-inch) lengths.

Remove the pork from the oven and lift out of the pan. Add the remaining ingredients to the pan, stir, then place the pork on top and return to the oven for a further 15–20 minutes, or until cooked through.

To serve, slice the pork fillet and serve with the rhubarb sauce.

Rabbit with prunes

Lapin aux pruneaux

Rabbit is a very lean meat that really benefits from being cooked with lots of liquid. Prunes are often served with rabbit as, once cooked, their deep, dark colour and silky texture marry well with it.

Preparation: **20 minutes, plus 1 hour soaking**

Cooking: **1 hour 20 minutes**

Serves: **4–6**

1 wild rabbit, jointed into 6 pieces

2 tbsp flour

sea salt and freshly ground black pepper

25g (1oz) butter

2 tbsp olive oil

300g (10oz) prunes, soaked in vegetable stock for 1 hour

200ml (7fl oz) white wine

Dust the rabbit joints all over with seasoned flour. Heat the butter and oil in a large flameproof casserole and sauté the rabbit joints until dark golden brown all over.

Remove the rabbit from the casserole and add the prunes – with their soaking stock – and the white wine to the casserole. Bring to the boil, then place the rabbit back in the casserole, cover with a lid and simmer for 1 hour over a very gentle heat, or until cooked through.

Serve the rabbit with the prune sauce spooned over.

Pears wrapped in walnut pastry

Chausson à la poire et aux noix

These were served to my children in the countryside around the Drôme, where fruit trees are abundant. They looked pretty and the boys loved them, so now we make them at home every autumn.

Preparation: **35 minutes, plus 1 hour 20 minutes chilling**

Cooking: **35–40 minutes**

Serves: **4**

4 firm pears with stalks

25g (1oz) plain flour

1–2 egg yolks, beaten

2 tbsp milk

25g (1oz) caster sugar

4 tbsp crème fraîche, to serve

Walnut pastry

50g (2oz) shelled walnuts

125g (4½oz) plain flour

75g (2½oz) cold butter, cut into small pieces

25g (1oz) caster sugar

1 large egg

For the walnut pastry, whizz the walnuts in a blender until finely ground. Combine with the flour in a bowl, add the butter and rub together quickly with your fingertips until the mixture resembles breadcrumbs. Add the sugar and mix through. Whisk the egg, then stir into the pastry mixture using a round-bladed knife to form a dough ball. Wrap in cling film and chill in the fridge for 1 hour.

Place the chilled pastry on a work surface and divide into 4. Roll out each piece into a circle whose diameter is twice the height of a pear so that it will be large enough to wrap and enclose the fruit.

Peel the pears and roll them in flour, then brush with beaten egg yolk. Place an individual pear in the middle of a circle of pastry and fold up the pastry around it, firmly shaping to encase it. Brush with a little milk and dust with caster sugar. Place on a baking sheet and repeat to wrap each pear in pastry.

Place the pears in the fridge and chill for 20 minutes before baking. Preheat the oven to 190°C/375°F/Gas 5.

Bake the pears for 20 minutes, then reduce the oven temperature to 160°C/325°F/Gas 3 and cook for a further 15–20 minutes until the pastry is crisp and golden. Serve warm with crème fraîche.

Domaine de Blancardy
Moules et Baucels (Hérault)
34190 Ganges

Telephone +33 (0)4 67 73 94 94

www.blancardy.com

Owner/chef: Laure Martial

Open 12noon – 1pm and 7.30 – 9pm

Closed all day Wednesday and Thursday lunchtime

Closed for 6 weeks a year – these times vary so it's advised that you always phone first to reserve a table.

Domaine de Blancardy

West of Nîmes and north of Montpellier calmly lies the amazing region of Cévennes-Mediterranean in the Languedoc-Roussillon. The land here is rich in produce, due to the sparkling waters that travel down from the hills on to wild and farmed plateaux. The Domaine de Blancardy has been in the Martial family since 1976, when Laure's parents moved here from Paris and restored this 12th-century fortified farm and added vines to the land. Laure and her husband, Alain, added ducks to the farm and Laure started to make foie gras and confit of duck and went on for 10 years to win the prestigious Hérault Gourmand awards in Montpellier. When asked why she no longer enters she laughs and says, 'After 10 years of winning there is no need!'

   Laure is charming and passionate about food and wine. Her grandmothers taught her to cook and her style is to use local produce, moving through the seasons. Her passion is the duck – 'the little bird pig' as she calls it – and every part is used to cook many different dishes. Since the couple gave up farming their own ducks, the best that could replace them have come from the Pyrénées. Laure prepares her own famous *confit de canard*, many and various foie gras, pâtés and jams in her 'laboratory' at the farm, and they are sold at the shop. In the autumn and winter she serves rabbit and *sanglier* (wild boar), which are shot in the surrounding woodlands, with wild mushrooms that have been gathered locally. All that Laure knows about mushrooms has been passed on to her by an English lady who lives in the area! Spring sees the addition of asparagus and the summer months feature melons and peaches, but all year round Laure's beloved duck is served. This place is both very traditional and modern, as Laure offers a full vegetarian menu, 'as it is required by so many guests', she laughs!

Snails in a pot

Cassolette d'escargots

This recipe delivers a rich and unusual little casserole of tasty snails, and Laure always puts it on the menu in the spring, as that is the new snail season; the garden is productive at that time, so the snails come out in abundance!

Preparation: **40 minutes**
Cooking: **1¼ hours**
Serves: **4**

2 lamb's or calf's feet

½ tsp dried Provençal herbs

2 carrots, diced

2 onions, thinly sliced

85g (3oz) lardons

250ml (9fl oz) white wine

about 48 prepared canned snails, without shells

salt and freshly ground black pepper

bunch of fresh parsley, chopped

4 slices toasted French bread, to serve

Wash the lamb's or calf's feet, place in a pan, cover with water and bring to the boil for 3 minutes. Drain and change the water, add the Provençal herbs and bring to the boil again, then cover and simmer for 30 minutes.

Add the carrots, onions, lardons and white wine and simmer for a further 1 hour. The liquid should reduce to a rich binding stock. Remove the lamb's or calf's feet and, when cool, pick the meat from the bone and cartilage, dice, and return to the pot.

Add the snails and seasoning, and bring to the boil. Add a little more wine, if needed, and simmer for 5 minutes. Divide between small individual pots, allowing about 12 snails per person. Garnish with chopped parsley and serve with slices of hot toasted French bread.

Preserved duck with potatoes

Confit de canard et pommes de terre

The confit used in this recipe can be made in advance and then stored in kilner jars, as long as the duck fat covers the meat. It can then be reheated as needed in an oven at 180°C/350°F/Gas 4 for 20 minutes. Laure makes a point of reminding me to reserve the fat as 'duck fat is precious'. Laure uses 5 litres (8 pints) of duck fat for her award-winning method although you can get by with just using 2 litres (3½ pints).

Preparation: **30 minutes, plus overnight marinating**

Cooking: **2 hours**

Serves: **6**

6 fat duck legs

6 tbsp sea salt

2 litres (3½ pints) duck fat

1 tbsp dried Provençal herbs

2kg (4½lb) large white potatoes, peeled

sea salt and freshly ground black pepper

4 garlic cloves, crushed

The night before you prepare this dish, rub the duck legs all over with sea salt, with extra on their skins, and refrigerate in a bowl. Preheat the oven to 150°C/300°F/Gas 2.

The following day, rinse the duck legs in cold running water and place in a large roasting pan. Cover with the duck fat and sprinkle over the herbs. Place in the oven and roast for 2 hours, taking care to ensure that the fat does not burn. The duck is cooked when the meat falls off the bone.

Meanwhile, slice the potatoes into thin rounds, place in a large non-stick frying pan or several smaller pans, and cover with some of the fat from the duck. Add seasoning and the garlic, then let the potatoes cook until golden, without touching them. Drain the potatoes when ready and serve with the duck.

Rabbit with mustard and tarragon

Lapin à la moutarde et estragon

Rabbit is very popular in France and frequently enjoyed. Laure likes to serve this dish in the autumn on a bed of fresh pasta or with sautéed mushrooms.

Preparation: **10 minutes**
Cooking: **45 minutes**
Serves: **6**

1 rabbit, about 1.8kg (4lb)
salt and freshly ground black pepper
25g (1oz) butter
10 sprigs of fresh tarragon
125ml (4fl oz) rosé wine
100ml (3½fl oz) water
3 tbsp strong mustard
3 tbsp tarragon mustard
500ml (18fl oz) crème fraîche

Joint the rabbit into small pieces and season. Melt the butter in a large shallow pan, add the rabbit and sauté over a high heat for about 10 minutes, until browned all over.

Set aside 2 sprigs of tarragon and add the leaves from the rest to the rabbit. Pour in the wine and simmer for a few minutes, then add the water, cover and simmer on a gentle heat for 15 minutes. Turn the rabbit pieces and cook for a further 15 minutes, or until cooked through.

Mix the two mustards together and then add the crème fraîche. Pour over the rabbit, stir well and simmer for 5 minutes. Scatter over the reserved tarragon leaves to garnish and serve.

Wild boar stew with flavours of the Cévennes

Daube de sanglier aux saveurs des Cévennes

In the autumn, when the shooting season begins, this dish is always on the menu at Blancardy and, as the air turns damp, it seems a great reason to enjoy this warming and delicious recipe. It needs to be marinated twice overnight so you need to start preparing it two days before serving.

Preparation: **1 hour, plus 2 overnights marinating**
Cooking: **1½ hours**
Serves: **6**

1.5kg (3lb 5oz) wild boar
1 onion
3 cloves
3 carrots, sliced
1 bouquet garni
75cl bottle *vin de pays* **red wine**
2 tbsp olive oil
1 pig's foot
salt and freshly ground black pepper
100ml (3½fl oz) water
75cl bottle Cabernet Sauvignon from Languedoc
100g (3½oz) mixed dried wild mushrooms
50g (2oz) chestnut flour
250g (9oz) peeled chestnuts

Two days before you prepare this dish, cut the boar into large cubes and place in a large bowl with the onion studded with cloves, the carrots, the bouquet garni and the vin de pays. Mix well, cover and leave to marinade for 24 hours.

The following day, drain the meat, reserving the marinade. Heat the oil in a large flameproof casserole and sauté the meat along with the pig's foot and seasoning until browned. Add the water and Cabernet Sauvignon and bring to a simmer.

Bring the reserved marinating wine to the boil in a pan, skim and strain into the casserole. Bring the contents of the casserole to the boil and boil for 5 minutes. Add the dried mushrooms, reduce the heat and simmer for 40 minutes. Remove from the heat, cool and store overnight in the fridge.

The final day, remove about 100ml (3½fl oz) of the stock from the meat and set aside. Gently heat the casserole, bringing it to a simmer, and cook for 40 minutes. Remove and discard the pig's foot.

Carefully mix the reserved stock into the chestnut flour so that you have a smooth, thin paste. Just before serving, mix this paste into the casserole with the peeled chestnuts. Stir well and boil for a few minutes to allow the juices to thicken. Season to taste and serve.

Peaches with mint

Pêches à la menthe

Towards Nîmes there are many peach orchards, and the variety that they grow are large, sweet and juicy. You can tell that they have ripened on the tree as the flesh comes away easily from the stone inside and they are so delicious.

Preparation: **30 minutes, plus chilling the syrup**

Serves: **6**

150g (5oz) caster sugar
4 white peaches
100ml (3½fl oz) mint syrup
26 fresh mint leaves
3 yellow peaches

Dissolve the sugar in 100ml (3½fl oz) hot water. Add 100ml (3½fl oz) very cold water and chill.

Peel one white peach, place in a blender with 200ml (7fl oz) water and the mint syrup, and blend until smooth. Place in the fridge.

Shred the mint leaves into fine ribbons, reserving 6 nice leaves for decorating. When the sugar syrup is chilled, add the shredded mint leaves to it. Peel the remaining peaches, slice into moons off the stone and place into the syrup.

Divide the peaches into 6 individual glasses, spoon over a little mint syrup and serve topped with a mint leaf.

Provence

Just mention Provence and immediately pleasant images of pungent lavender fields, shimmering plains of olive groves, and bistros serving fresh and simple food spring to mind. It is also renowned for its wonderful produce: tomatoes, purple garlic, courgettes, olives, olive oil, basil, honey, peppers, peaches and apricots and, in the winter months, truffles and mushrooms. In the summer the food is fresh and vegetable-led, yet in the cold winter months, when the mistral storms across the region, warming pots of meat like *daube de boeuf* (beef stew), are savoured. All this produce may be enjoyed with a glass or two of wine from the famed vineyards of the Rhône valley. Further down in Provence the land is covered with vines that were planted during World War I so that every soldier could be given his daily ration of a litre of wine. The Luberon area is well known for its rolling hills, which are home to a variety of wild game that is enjoyed in season, in dishes such as *civet* (wild boar stew). The markets in Provence are a real treat: not only is the food good, but there is also an abundance of baskets and pretty, traditional, Provençal-style prints in an array of hot colours. Often I think of eastern Provence as a melting pot of French and Italian cookery – lots of ingredients, such as risotto rice and polenta, are shared, and what is a delicious *pissaldière* in France is a pizza in Italy. Provence is a region where you will be tempted at every corner to enjoy delicious and tasty food.

Green olive and garlic tapenade

Tapenade d'olives vertes et ail

I just love bistros that serve surprise foodie delights with drinks; it's a really good way of taking the urgency out of ordering and allows you more time to savour the menu and make your choice. In the south, where olives are abundant, it is very normal to be served a little bowl of house tapenade while you wait for your order to be taken.

Preparation: **10 minutes**

Serves: **4**

300g (10oz) pitted green olives

3 garlic cloves, crushed

bunch of fresh coriander

150ml (¼ pint) olive oil

1 tbsp red wine vinegar

freshly ground black pepper

slices of toasted bread or bread sticks, to serve

Place the olives, garlic and coriander in a blender and whizz until diced. Keep the motor running and slowly pour in the olive oil, then add the vinegar and pepper to season. It's up to you how smooth you make your tapenade – it can be roughly chopped or puréed to a paste.

Serve with slices of toasted bread or bread sticks for dipping. The tapenade can be stored, covered with a thin layer of olive oil, in the fridge for up to 3 days.

Butternut squash soup with pine nuts and argon oil

Soupe de courge à l'huile d'argon et pignons

The silky-smooth flesh of the butternut infused with sweet, nutty argon oil and butter-bursting pine nuts make this soup irresistible. Argon oil comes from Morocco, where it is collected and produced by Berber women. It is available from good delicatessans. Alternatively, you could substitute a fine extra virgin olive oil.

Preparation: **20 minutes**

Cooking: **30 minutes**

Serves: **4**

2 onions, diced

1 garlic clove, crushed

1 tbsp olive oil

1–1.25kg (2lb 4oz–2lb 12oz) butternut squash, peeled, deseeded and chopped

200ml (7fl oz) white wine

700ml (7fl oz) chicken stock

sea salt and freshly ground black pepper

bunch of fresh parsley, chopped

50g (2oz) pine nuts, toasted

2 tsp argon oil or extra virgin olive oil

Sauté the onions and garlic gently in the olive oil in a medium saucepan. Add the squash, along with the wine and stock, bring to the boil, then simmer for 20 minutes until the squash is soft.

Blend the soup with a hand-held blender or food processor until silky smooth and season to taste. Serve sprinkled with chopped parsley, toasted pine nuts and a thin drizzle of oil.

Lamb shanks with broad beans

Souris d'agneau aux fèves

This recipe is inspired by a memorable meal that I ate in the south of France using fantastic spring lamb and early season broad beans. It's one that I just had to share.

Preparation: **45 minutes**

Cooking: **1 hour 20 minutes**

Serves: **4**

1 tbsp olive oil

4 lamb shanks

sea salt and freshly ground black pepper

2 red onions, sliced

2 garlic cloves, chopped

1 fresh bouquet garni (sprig each of parsley and thyme and a bay leaf)

400ml (14fl oz) white wine

400g (14oz) new potatoes

400g (14oz) shelled broad beans, individually skinned (*see* Cook's note, right)

2 tbsp chopped fresh mint

3 tbsp crème fraîche

Preheat the oven to 180°C/350°F/Gas 4. Lightly oil a roasting tin, add the lamb shanks and season, then place in the oven to roast for 20 minutes. Add the onions, garlic and bouquet garni to the roasting tin and roast for a further 20 minutes.

Add the wine and new potatoes to the lamb, mix well with the juices and return to the oven for a further 20 minutes.

Add the prepared beans and return to the oven for 10 minutes.

When the lamb is cooked through, remove from the roasting tin and keep warm. Place the tin directly on the stove top and bring the juices to a simmer. Stir in the chopped mint and crème fraîche. Serve the shanks in wide bowls and ladle in the vegetables and juice.

Cook's note

To skin fresh broad beans, plunge them into a pan of boiling water for 4 minutes, then drain and peel off the skins. If using frozen beans they can be peeled once defrosted.

Pigeon with garden salad

Palombes et salade du jardin

This is called 'garden salad' as in the Provençal countryside most people grow their own salad leaves, which are bursting with assorted hot, peppery flavours. In French markets you can also buy freshly picked, small young leaves called **mâche**, *which make the individual lettuce seem dull in comparison; they offer crunch and a variety of lovely flavours. This salad makes a fantastic starter or, in double quantities, a great main course.*

Preparation: **15 minutes**

Cooking: **4 minutes**

Serves: **4**

4 tbsp olive oil, plus extra for frying

4 pigeon breasts

2 tbsp red wine vinegar

sea salt and freshly ground black pepper

pinch of sugar

300g (10oz) *mâche* or mixed salad leaves

½ pomegranate, seeds picked out

Heat some oil in a frying pan and cook the pigeon breasts for 2 minutes on each side. Remove and leave to rest for 5 minutes.

Place the 4 tbsp olive oil in a large bowl with the vinegar, whisk, then add seasoning and sugar. Add the *mâche* or mixed salad leaves and toss in the dressing.

Place the salad on serving plates. Finely carve the pigeon breasts, place on top of the salad and serve scattered with pomegranate seeds.

Calf's liver with poached baby beetroots and thyme

Foie de veau, betteraves et thym

This is a wonderfully easy dish to be relished by anyone who enjoys calf's liver. It works very well as the liver and beetroot both have such silky textures, which complement each other.

Preparation: **10 minutes**
Cooking: **1 hour 5 minutes**
Serves: **4**

400g (14oz) baby beetroots, trimmed
85g (3oz) butter
bunch of fresh thyme
juice of ½ lemon
salt and freshly ground black pepper
4 x 175g (6oz) thin slices calf's liver
75ml (2½fl oz) Madeira wine

Simmer the baby beetroots in a pan of water for 1 hour until soft when a knife is inserted. Drain and, when cool enough to handle, peel by squeezing gently; the skins should slip off.

Cut the beetroots in half and place in a large pan with 25g (1oz) of the butter, the bunch of thyme, lemon juice and seasoning. Simmer gently for 5 minutes.

Meanwhile, melt the remaining butter in a large frying pan and sauté the liver for 2 minutes on each side for rare, 3 minutes on each side for medium and 4 minutes on each side for well done (which is, in my opinion, a sin!). Transfer to a dish.

Deglaze the frying pan with the Madeira and serve the liver with the beetroot, drizzled with a spoonful of the Madeira pan juices.

Veal chops with onion compote

Côtes de veau à la compote d'oignons

Veal needs careful cooking as it does not have much natural marbling fat running through it, so do baste as frequently as possible when preparing this bistro dish.

Preparation: **25 minutes**
Cooking: **1 hour 10 minutes**
Serves: **4**

4 tbsp olive oil
4 red onions, finely sliced
4 garlic cloves, crushed in their skins
sprig of fresh rosemary
bunch of fresh thyme
200ml (7fl oz) white wine
50ml (scant 2fl oz) sherry vinegar
sea salt and freshly ground black pepper
4 loin veal chops
100ml (3½fl oz) chicken stock

Preheat the oven to 180°C/350°F/Gas 4. Heat half the oil in an ovenproof pan and fry the onions until just softened, stirring frequently. Add the garlic, rosemary, thyme, wine, vinegar and seasoning and simmer over a low heat.

In another pan, heat the remaining oil and brown the veal chops for 5 minutes on each side. Remove and add to the onion pan.

Add the stock to the pan used for the veal and simmer rapidly to deglaze, scraping up any meaty bits with a wooden spoon.

Pour the stock over the chops, then place them in the oven in the ovenproof pan to braise for 1 hour 10 minutes, or until cooked through. Baste from time to time to keep the chops moist and give them a lovely golden colour.

Provençal slow-cooked beef

Estouffade de bœuf à la Provençale

It's the slow cooking of this dish that gives it such a rich, tasty dark sauce, so do not make it in a hurry and, if possible, prepare it a day in advance, chill, then reheat to make a superb beef casserole.

Preparation: **30 minutes**
Cooking: **2 hours 35 minutes**
Serves: **4**

50g (2oz) butter

4 tbsp olive oil

1.2kg (2lb 12oz) braising beef, cubed

8 shallots, halved

115g (4oz) lardons

50g (2oz) plain flour

750ml *vin de table* red wine

2 garlic cloves, chopped

bunch of fresh thyme

2 bay leaves

sea salt and freshly ground black pepper

200g (7oz) button mushrooms

1 large aubergine, chopped

bunch of fresh parsley, chopped

Preheat the oven to 160°C/325°F/Gas 3. Melt the butter with half the oil in a flameproof casserole, add the cubed beef and sauté until well browned. Remove the meat from the casserole using a draining spoon and set aside.

Add the shallots and lardons to the casserole and sauté until golden. Remove and stir the flour into the fat left in the casserole to make a roux. Slowly stir in the wine to make a smooth sauce.

Return the beef, lardons and shallots to the casserole, along with the garlic, thyme, bay leaves and seasoning. Cover and place in the oven to cook for 1 hour.

Sauté the button mushrooms and chopped aubergine for 8 minutes in a pan over a medium heat in the remaining oil. Stir into the casserole and cook for a further hour.

Spoon off any excess fat that has risen to the top, using a metal spoon. Stir in the chopped parsley and serve.

casse
croûte

le jus des pommes   le verre 1
le vin   le verre 1
le pain   la portion 0,50
l'apéritif   le verre 1,50
la tapenade   le
la châtaigne en pâté   la portion 3,50
la salade   la portion 3,50
l'omelette   la portion 3,50
le fromage   la portion 3,50
le dessert   la portion 3,50
le café, le thé   la portion 3,50
                                          le verre 1€

La Colline
Route des Crêtes
83230 Bormes les Mimosas

Telephone +33 (0)4 94 64 82 87

Owner/chef: Josette Olivier

*Open 1st week before Easter –
end of August*

Lunch every day

Dinner July and August only

La Colline

Travel away from the coast up into the mountains, past the expensive village of Bormes, and then turn right and travel along the road overlooking the Mediterranean to the islands of Hyères. Turn into a little track and you land at this amazing little summer secret for those who want a restful and simple, fresh, homemade, organic meal with almost everything produced on the farm. The sun shines long and warm here and perhaps it makes the egg yolks a vivid orange as both the omelettes and the crème caramel have a rich golden glow. The drinks on the menu are homemade apple juice and tisanes from garden mint and verbena, so if you wish for some wine, be sure to bring your own.

Just before World War I, Olivier's grandmother bought the hill, gave each of her children a plot of land and life started for the elegant Josette. It is something of a retreat up here and the family lives by the seasons. They see the winter as being 'the most important season as everything is able to rest to start life again in the spring'. This little restaurant started 10 years ago and the produce served is from the farm. It is a very simple menu: *soupe au pistou*, tapenade, omelettes, salad and *chèvre* at lunchtime, and in the evening for one month only, it's Josette's speciality of goat cooked in white wine. When this runs out she buys in lamb.

The desserts are *clafoutis*, using the farm's fruits as they ripen, and a custard cream served with fruit using the goats' milk. Nothing travels far except the diners! Josette must be 70 or 80 and she has some help, but generally likes to cook herself at her family kitchen farmhouse range. If the weather is not good you can sit and eat at her kitchen table. The warmth and attention to simplicity that has gone into this place is amazing and after cooking Josette still finds time to make her famous goats' cheese and marmalade, which she sells in the market at Bormes les Mimosas.

Plum tart

Clafoutis

A really simple dessert that makes good use of the abundance of fruit in season. Josette never stones the fruit as she believes that the stones add to the flavour. It also means that the fruits are cooked whole in the batter, intensifying their individual taste.

Preparation: **20 minutes**

Cooking: **50 minutes**

Serves: **6**

20g (scant 1oz) butter, for greasing

800g (1lb 12oz) mirabelle plums or other whole stone fruits (such as fresh apricots, cherries, or prunes)

50g (2oz) plain flour

85g (3oz) caster sugar

pinch of salt

4 eggs

2 egg yolks

650ml (1 pint 2fl oz) goats' milk (or half goats' milk and half water)

icing sugar or caster sugar, to sprinkle

Preheat the oven to 190°C/375°F/Gas 5. Butter a shallow-sided 2 litre (3½ pint) dish and place the fruit in it.

Place the flour, sugar and salt in a mixing bowl, stir together and make a well in the centre. Beat the eggs, egg yolks and milk together slowly, then pour into the bowl and beat constantly to make a smooth batter.

Pour the batter over the fruit, then place in the oven to bake for 30 minutes. Reduce the heat to 150°C/300°F/Gas 2 and bake for a further 20 minutes until golden on top and set in the middle. Sprinkle with a little icing sugar or caster sugar and serve immediately.

Josette's lamb casserole in white wine

Casserole d'agneau au vin blanc de Josette

At the start of the season, Josette serves this dish made with her goats and when she has used this supply it's replaced with local lamb. Josette's tip, which I love, is to grill the meat after marinating. As she says, 'This allows the fat to drip away.' Serve the meat and juices in bowls with minted new potatoes.

Preparation: **5 minutes, plus overnight marinating**

Cooking: **1 hour 20 minutes**

Serves: **4**

1.5kg (3lb 5oz) pieces of lamb or goat, on the bone

4 shallots, diced

4 juniper berries, crushed

bunch of fresh thyme

400ml (14fl oz) white wine

1 tsp ground nutmeg

salt and freshly ground black pepper

Place the meat, shallots, crushed juniper berries, thyme, white wine, nutmeg and seasoning in a large casserole. Mix well, then cover and leave to marinate overnight in the fridge.

Preheat the grill to hot. Drain the meat from the marinade, place on a grill rack and grill for 10 minutes on both sides – this allows the fat to drip away. Preheat the oven to 180°C/350°F/Gas 4.

Return the meat to the marinade and place in the oven to cook gently for 1 hour, or until the meat is tender and cooked through. Serve immediately.

milk pudding

Dessert au lait de chèvre et caramel

A gentle-flavoured, lightly set milk pudding that is lovely served with seasonal fruit, jam or compote.

Preparation: **10 minutes**

Cooking: **50 minutes**

Serves: **6**

1 litre (1¼ pints) goats' milk

6 very fresh eggs

150g (5oz) caster sugar

jam or fruit, to serve

Preheat the oven to 180°C/350°F/Gas 4. Heat the milk in a pan until warm. Whisk the eggs and sugar together, then slowly whisk in the warm milk. Pour into a 2 litre (3½ pint) shallow, rectangular ceramic dish.

Carefully place the dish in a bain-marie (a larger dish or roasting tin filled with boiling water, coming about two thirds of the way up the sides of the ceramic dish). Place in the oven and cook for 5 minutes, then reduce the heat to 160°C/325°F/Gas 3 and cook for a further 45 minutes, or until set to the touch.

Serve cut in squares with a little jam or fruit.

Le Bistrot du Paradou
57 avenue Vallée des Baux
13520 Paradou

Telephone +33 (0)4 90 54 32 70

paquit2002@hotmail.com

Owners/chefs: Jean-Louis and
Mireille Pons

*Open Winter lunch only Tuesday –
Friday and Saturday dinner only*

*Summer lunch and dinner Monday –
Saturday*

Le Bistrot du Paradou

In the little village of Paradou you will find Le Bistrot du Paradou, a lovely French building with classic, blue shutters next to the most handsome plane tree, under which you can sit and sip a cooling aperitif. Walk inside and the room is large and cool with stone walls and a dark-beamed ceiling. Already I can feel my heart skipping a beat; this looks good. The tables are a mixture of marble and large wooden, almost refectory-style, and are laid with cutlery, large plates with green or red napkins, a bottle of olive oil and wine. The room comfortably seats 55 covers. There is a set menu that includes wine, specially bottled for the bistro from a local vineyard, and coffee. Faithful clients phone for the next week's menu and then make their reservation according to what is being served. This is an amazing place with a very simple but classic formula: two waiters look after the whole room and the charming owner Jean-Louis greets each customer personally and then sits to enjoy lunch with friends. It is popular with the locals, farmers, businessmen and travellers. The mayor was even dining there when I had lunch! Mireille Pons, Jean-Louis's wife, heads up the open-plan kitchen and selects the set menu every week. Both Jean-Louis and Mireille are very relaxed, and so they should be; on the wall is a large collage of photographs of Hollywood's 'A' list munching down at this great bistro.

Visit this place and you will be charmed by the attention to simple details and the quality of the delicious bistro food that Mireille sends out of her kitchen. Then, when you have eaten your way through three courses, a handsome cheeseboard is delivered and it is suggested that they leave it with you and you help yourself – that is true, indulgent, glutinous heaven to me!

Barigoule artichokes

Artichauts à la barigoule

In the summer months when small, young artichokes are in season and abundant, try this classic recipe with a twist. The violet artichoke is native to Provence and, as it is so young, will have hardly produced any choke, making its preparation easier and quicker. The wine and herbs add flavour and this dish is often served as a starter or alongside a simple roast leg of lamb, or Bresse chicken (see page 172).

Preparation: **30 minutes**
Cooking: **50 minutes**
Serves: **4–6**

juice of 1 lemon
12 small purple artichokes
3 tbsp olive oil
2 white onions, diced
100ml (3½fl oz) white wine
3 carrots, cut into small sticks
5 garlic cloves, chopped
few sprigs of fresh thyme
125g (4½oz) peas

Fill a large bowl with water and add the lemon juice. Cut off the top of each artichoke and peel away the outer tougher leaves then peel the stem and trim to approximately 5cm (2 inches) in length. Use a teaspoon to remove the choke, if there is any. Place in the acidulated water to prevent them going black.

Heat the oil in a saucepan, add the onion and artichoke hearts and cook for 6–7 minutes, stirring all the time. Pour in the white wine, increase the heat and cook rapidly to evaporate the liquid.

Add the carrots, garlic and thyme and enough water to come half-way up the artichokes. Lower the heat and simmer gently for 40 minutes, adding a little extra water if needed.

Just before serving, add the peas and cook for 1 minute. Serve with the roast Bresse chicken.

Provençal aubergines

Aubergines à la Provençale

This is a staple at Le Bistrot du Paradou. I am told by Mireille that almost every traveller who comes to Provence wants to eat this classic dish of aubergines bathed in a rich tomato sauce. These aubergines absorb less oil on frying as they are salted, drained and rinsed before cooking. In Provence, basil is very much part of cooking and is often blended into olive oil and then drizzled abundantly over vegetables, giving them a delicious, summery flavour.

Preparation: **30 minutes, plus 1 hour salting**

Cooking: **30 minutes**

Serves: **4**

4 aubergines

salt and freshly ground black pepper

1 white onion, finely diced

3 dsp olive oil

2 x 300g cans chopped tomatoes

bunch of fresh basil

sunflower oil, for frying

basil oil, for drizzling

Peel the aubergines and cut into slices lengthways. Score the flesh lengthways, place the aubergines on kitchen paper, sprinkle with salt and leave in a cool place for 1 hour.

Sauté the onion in 2 dsp of the oil for 10 minutes. Add the tomatoes and stew over a gentle heat for 20 minutes. Reserve a few good basil leaves for the garnish, then chop the remainder and add to the sauce with the remaining olive oil. Season to taste.

Rinse the salt from the aubergines and pat them dry with kitchen paper. Heat some sunflower oil in a large pan and fry the aubergines on each side until golden. Drain on kitchen paper. Serve with spoonfuls of the tomato stew and decorate with the reserved basil leaves and a drizzle of basil oil.

Bresse chicken

Poulet de Bresse et artichauts à la barigoule

These are the AOC (Appellation d'origine contrôlée) of chickens and the only ones that Mireille will allow into her kitchen: the simplicity of this recipe is down to the great taste of these chickens and they go so well with a delicious artichoke heart stew.

Preparation: **20 minutes**
Cooking: **1½ hours**
Serves: **4–6**

2 garlic cloves
few sprigs of fresh thyme
1 x Bresse chicken, about 2kg (4½lb)
4 thin strips salt pork or bacon
salt and freshly ground black pepper
3 tbsp groundnut oil
Barigoule artichokes, to serve

Preheat the oven to 160°C/325°F/Gas 3. Place the garlic and thyme inside the chicken, cover the breast with the thin strips of salt pork or bacon and sprinkle with seasoning.

Place the chicken in a roasting tin and pour over the oil. Roast for 1½ hours, basting with the juices from time to time. To check the chicken is cooked, push a skewer into the thigh at the thickest point. If the juices run clear, it is done; if not, give it another 5 minutes, then test again.

Serve with Barigoule artichokes (*see* page 168).

Leg or shoulder of lamb with ratatouille and puréed potato

Gigot ou épaule d'agneau, ratatouille et purée de pommes de terre

This lamb is traditionally cooked to be served in the true French style of rare. However, this isn't to everybody's taste, so I've given directions for all degrees of doneness below.

Preparation: **5 minutes**
Cooking: **about 1 hour**
Serves: **4**

1 boned leg or shoulder of lamb, about 900g (2lb)

8 garlic cloves, crushed

4 sprigs of fresh thyme

3 tbsp groundnut oil

salt and freshly ground black pepper

Puréed potato
500g (1lb 2oz) floury potatoes, peeled

250ml (9fl oz) milk

150g (5oz) butter

Ratatouille
2 onions, diced

2 tbsp olive oil

1 green pepper, 1 red pepper and 1 yellow pepper, deseeded and chopped

300g can chopped tomatoes

bunch of fresh thyme

3 garlic cloves, finely chopped

4 courgettes, diced

4 aubergines, cubed

Preheat the oven to 160°C/325°F/Gas 3. Place the lamb in a roasting pan, add the garlic and thyme and rub the meat with 2 tablespoons of the groundnut oil and seasoning. Place in the oven to roast, basting from time to time with the cooking juices, until cooked through. Allow 20 minutes per 450g (1lb) plus 20 minutes for rare, 25 minutes per 450g (1lb) plus 25 minutes for medium and 30 minutes per 450g (1lb) plus 30 minutes for well done.

Meanwhile, make the puréed potato. Place the potatoes in cold water with a little salt and bring to the boil. Reduce the heat and simmer for 18 minutes, until soft. Bring the milk to the boil.

Pass the potatoes through a potato sieve, if you have one, or beat with a hand-held electric mixer. Add the hot milk and cold butter and beat until creamy and blended. Season to taste.

For the ratatouille, place the onions in a saucepan with half the olive oil and sauté for 5 minutes. Add the peppers to the pan and sauté for 5 minutes. Add the tomatoes, thyme, garlic and seasoning. Mix together well and cook gently for 20 minutes.

Fry the courgettes in the remaining olive oil until just golden, then drain on kitchen paper. Fry the aubergine in the remaining groundnut oil until just golden, then drain on kitchen paper.

Add the courgettes and aubergines to the pepper mixture and gently simmer for 30 minutes.

Serve the lamb accompanied by the puréed potato and ratatouille.

Côte d'Azur

Côte d'Azur is part of Provence, but is often referred to separately as it is the coastline that runs along the Mediterranean Sea and the region takes its exotic name from the blueness of this sea. The Côte d'Azur is a summer playground for the rich and beautiful, and the season starts in spring with the Cannes Film Festival, which draws a host of major 'A' list stars. The large cities of Nice, Cannes, Monaco and Marseilles are either loved or not so loved by many as at the height of the season they are full to the brim with holiday-makers, but visit in spring or autumn and you will find a gentler and calmer environment in which to relax and enjoy their natural beauty, although in the midst of winter many places will be closed. Many of the ingredients used here are similar to those in Provence, but with the added abundance of seafood, cooked in every way. Visit any market and you will see fish so fresh from the sea that they are still moving on the stalls! Most of the fish are sweet and small with *rouget* (red mullet) and *loup* (sea bass) being the most common. They are often simply grilled drizzled with local olive oil and a squeeze of lemon. The more classic dishes are *bouillabaisse* from Marseilles and *bourride*, which is served with *rouille*, a tasty garlic and chilli mayonnaise that is spooned on top along with croûtons. In the heat of the summer beautiful salads and tasty, grilled vegetables are enjoyed, dressed with quality olive oils.

Courgettes with goats' cheese, chilli and pine nuts

Courgettes au chèvre, piment et pignons

In the summer months, when courgettes are abundant, bistros cook them in a variety of ways; this is one of my favourites. Serve as a lunchtime dish or with a simply cooked fish fillet or barbecued meat.

Preparation: **20 minutes**

Cooking: **5 minutes**

Serves: **4**

6 courgettes, long or rugby-ball shaped

1 tbsp olive oil, plus a little extra for dressing

1–2 fresh red chillies, deseeded and diced

1 garlic clove, crushed

85g (3oz) pine nuts, toasted

125g (4½oz) soft goats' cheese

large bunch of fresh parsley, chopped

Chop the courgettes into irregular chunks. Heat the oil in a large frying pan, add the courgettes and stir-fry on a high heat for 3–4 minutes until just golden on the outside but crisp in the middle.

Add the chilli and garlic and cook for a further minute, then remove from the heat.

Scatter with the toasted pine nuts, crumbled goats' cheese and chopped parsley, then dress with a little olive oil before serving.

Goats' cheese preserved in oil and herbs

Crottins de chèvre marinés à l'huile et aux herbes

When you find a goats' cheese you like, buy several, then prepare them in this way to turn a simple salad, pasta or pizza dish into something extra special.

Preparation: 15 minutes, plus 1 week minimum storage (they will keep for up to 3 months, developing a more intense flavour)

Serves: **4**

350ml (12fl oz) olive oil

2 sprigs of fresh rosemary

2 bay leaves

2 sprigs of fresh thyme

2 garlic cloves

1 fresh red chilli, seeds left in, sliced

6 black peppercorns

4 goats' cheese crottins, approx 5–10 days old

Heat the oil in a pan until warm, then remove from the heat. Add the rosemary, bay leaves, thyme, garlic cloves, red chilli and peppercorns, stir and then leave to cool completely.

Place the goats' cheese in an airtight container and pour over the herb oil. Top up with a little extra oil if needed, so that the crottins are totally covered. Leave to steep for a minimum of 1 week in a cool, dark place.

Use the goats' cheese as wished in salads, pasta or pizza. Reserve the oil and use again for a salad dressing.

Baked spider crab

Araignée de mer au four

Many believe spider crab to be the finest of all crabs. It is not always easily available, so if you see it in the shops, buy it then and there and cook up this recipe. You can then make your own mind up as to its taste and superiority!

Preparation: **1 hour, plus cooling**

Cooking: **35 minutes**

Serves: **2**

2 spider crabs, about 1.5–2kg (3lb 5oz–4½lb)

150g (5oz) extra brown crabmeat

4 spring onions, finely sliced

1 garlic clove, finely chopped

bunch of fresh parsley, chopped

1 fresh red chilli, deseeded and diced

juice and grated zest of 2 lemons

sea salt and freshly ground black pepper

3 tbsp crème fraîche

2 tbsp white wine

150g (5oz) fresh white breadcrumbs

Heat a large pan of boiling water, plunge in the crabs, cover and boil for 15 minutes. Drain and cool the crabs. When cool enough to handle, break off the legs, crack open and remove the white meat.

To open the main body of the crab, lay it on its back and insert a sharp knife, then twist to separate the two shells. Spoon out the meat and add it to the leg meat. Remove the dead man's fingers (feathery gills) and discard, then wash the crab shell. Patiently pick out all the white meat from the base shell with the help of a crab pick. Add to the other meats along with the extra brown crabmeat.

Preheat the oven to 180°C/350°F/Gas 4. Add the spring onions, garlic, parsley, chilli, lemon zest and juice and seasoning to the crabmeat and mix well.

Mix in the crème fraîche, white wine and half the breadcrumbs, spoon back into the washed crab shell and sprinkle with the remaining breadcrumbs. Place on a baking sheet and bake for 20 minutes. If necessary, brown the crab under the grill before serving so that the breadcrumb topping is golden.

Salt cod brandade

Brandade de morue

*This pounded combination of salted fish, olive oil, garlic and cream is a speciality of Provence and the Languedoc. Each region has its own unique version; some say 'no' to garlic, others use a purée of potatoes and some add truffles! The word **brandar** means to stir and stirring is certainly needed for this recipe!*

Preparation: **25 minutes, plus 2 days soaking**

Cooking: **45 minutes**

Serves: **4**

500g (1lb 2oz) salt cod (*morue*)

200ml (7fl oz) milk

200g (7oz) potatoes, peeled and chopped

6 garlic cloves, skinned

250ml (9fl oz) olive oil

100ml (3½fl oz) double cream

freshly ground white pepper

salt, to taste (optional)

toasted bread, to serve

First soak the fish in cold water for 2 days, changing the water as frequently as possible or leave a slow running tap trickling into the bowl of soaking fish.

Place the fish in a pan with the milk and simmer for 20 minutes over a low heat. Carefully lift out the fish using a draining spoon and, when cool enough to handle, flake the fish, discarding the skin and any bones.

Add the chopped potatoes, garlic and oil to the warm milk and gently simmer for 20 minutes, or until the potatoes are soft. Drain, reserving the milk.

In a saucepan, beat the fish with a wooden spoon until creamed. Pass the cooked potatoes and garlic through a potato ricer (or mash well until really smooth) and add to the creamed fish. Add a little of the reserved milk stock and beat well. Add the double cream and season with white pepper, beating over a low heat. Check if you need salt and add if wished. Beat until creamy and smooth.

Serve warm in little pots with toasted bread.

Niçoise of sea bream

Daurade à la Niçoise

This is a dish that takes its name from the region around Nice and in many bistros you will be served fish or meat that is cooked à la Niçoise. There is also, of course, the famous Niçoise salad, which consists of quality vegetables from the area and tuna.

Preparation: **20 minutes**

Cooking: **20 minutes**

Serves: **4**

4 tbsp olive oil

4 large tomatoes, skinned and chopped

4 garlic cloves, chopped

4 anchovy fillets, finely chopped

375g (13oz) French green beans, trimmed

250g (9oz) small new potatoes, cooked and sliced

sea salt and freshly ground black pepper

4 sea bream fillets, each about 175g (6oz)

85g (3oz) pitted Niçoise olives, chopped

fresh basil leaves

Preheat the oven to 190°C/375°F/Gas 5. Place the olive oil, chopped tomatoes, garlic, anchovies, green beans and potatoes in a large bowl, add seasoning and mix well, coating all the ingredients in the oil.

Put the vegetable mixture in a roasting tin, cover with foil and place in the oven to bake for 10 minutes.

Remove the foil and place the sea bream fillets on top of the vegetables. Bake for a further 8–10 minutes.

Serve topped with chopped olives and torn basil leaves.

Lemon tart

Tarte au citron

Think sweet, crumbling pastry filled with rich, creamy citrus custard. The two marry together like heaven in this delicious, classic dessert, which is served all over France. There are many variations; mine is the marbling in the custard, achieved by swirling in the last bit of cream during cooking.

Preparation: **40 minutes, plus 1 hour for chilling the pastry**

Cooking: **1 hour**

Serves: **4–6**

Pastry

150g (5oz) plain flour

75g (2½oz) cold butter, cut into small pieces

25g (1oz) caster sugar

1 large egg

Filling

2 eggs

50g (2oz) caster sugar

175ml (6fl oz) double cream

juice and grated zest of 2 lemons

sifted icing sugar, for dusting

For the pastry, place the flour and butter in a bowl and rub together quickly using your fingertips until the mixture resembles the texture of breadcrumbs. Add the sugar and mix through. Whisk the egg, then stir into the pastry mix using a round-bladed knife to form a dough ball. Wrap in cling film and chill in the fridge for 1 hour.

Preheat the oven to 190°C/375°F/Gas 5. Place the chilled pastry on a work surface, press out with the heel of your hand, then roll out to fit a 23cm (9-inch) loose-based flan tin. Do not stretch the pastry to fit. Trim away the excess from around the edge, then prick the base with a fork. Line the pastry case with baking parchment and fill with baking beans, then cook for 20 minutes.

Reduce the oven temperature to 160°C/325°F/Gas 3. Remove the beans and baking parchment and return the flan case to the oven to bake for a further 10 minutes.

Meanwhile, make the filling. Whisk the eggs and caster sugar, then add all but 2 tablespoons of the cream, and the lemon juice and zest, and mix together. Pour into the prepared pastry case and cook for 10 minutes. Swirl in the remaining cream to create a marbled effect, then continue to cook for a further 20 minutes until the filling is just set.

Leave to cool and dust with sifted icing sugar before serving.

Blackcurrant sorbet with cassis

Sorbet au cassis

The delicacy of sorbet packed with tart, strong-flavoured fruit is fantastic on a screamingly hot summer's day.

Preparation: **25 minutes, plus freezing**

Cooking: **10 minutes**

Serves: **4**

175g (6oz) caster sugar

175ml (6fl oz) water

500g (1lb 2oz) fresh blackcurrants

juice of ½ lemon

2 tbsp crème de cassis

1 egg white, lightly whisked

Gently heat the caster sugar with the water in a pan. When the sugar has dissolved, increase the heat and boil the mixture for 2 minutes.

Place the blackcurrants in a blender and whizz to a purée. Add the prepared syrup, lemon juice and crème de cassis to the blackcurrant purée and whizz again.

If you have an ice cream-making machine, transfer the mixture into it and follow the instructions. If not, tip the mixture into a freezerproof container, place in the freezer for 15 minutes and then blend again. Repeat until the mixture takes on a soft sorbet consistency. (If it will fit, you can put the blender bowl in the freezer, rather than transferring the mixture to a plastic container.)

Add the egg white, blend and return to the freezer. Eat within 24 hours. (It becomes too icy if left for longer.)

La Merenda
4 rue Raoul Bosio
06000 Nice

No telephone

Chef: Dominique le Stanc

*Open Monday to Friday 12noon –
2pm and 7pm – around 10pm*

La Merenda

In *vieux* (old) Nice, just a few roads back from the seafront, sits this small, compact and simple bistro serving rustic, peasant Niçoise food at its very best. The chef Dominique le Stanc is a gentle and quiet man who left the amazing Négresco Hotel's Chantecler restaurant as he felt he was losing touch with food and just organizing his brigade of chefs. So 11 years ago he opted out and brought La Merenda. He changed nothing from the previous owner except the paintings on the wall. Dominique did not have to buy replacements; local, well-known artists gave him new artwork – maybe in return for a few meals!

This tiny restaurant is simply run with two lunch and dinner sittings on a first come, first served basis, as they do not have a phone. Dominique's wife Danielle helps with the table service and Dominique personally cooks each customer's food with calm, passion and pleasure. Every day his deputy chef prepares food and a woman comes for just a couple of hours every morning to wash salad and prepare vegetables. This is a very small team running an internationally acclaimed restaurant serving simple and honest food. Dominique cycles around the corner to the old market in the square to buy his produce and has fishermen who bring him the much-famed poutine fish. This he lightly poaches in water and serves with fresh bread and chopped garlic or simply marinates, as the mood takes him when the fisherman brings in a catch.

Courgette flower fritters

Beignets de fleurs de courgettes

When summer is in mid-flow, courgettes grow abundantly. This is a great way of cooking the flowers, and the addition of garlic and parsley is an example of how Dominique likes to put his twist on dishes.

Preparation: **10 minutes, plus 20 minutes resting**

Cooking: **about 10 minutes**

Serves: **4**

250g (9oz) flour

250ml (9fl oz) olive oil

1 egg

25ml (1fl oz) water

¼ bunch of fresh parsley, finely chopped

3 garlic cloves, finely chopped

oil, for deep-fat frying

12–16 courgette flowers (depending on size)

sea salt, to serve

Whisk together the flour, oil and egg with the water. Add the parsley and garlic to the batter, then leave to rest for 20 minutes.

Preheat the oil in a deep-fat fryer, set at 180°C/350°F. Dip the courgette flowers into the batter in batches and fry for 2–3 minutes. Remove and place on kitchen paper to drain. Serve sprinkled with a little sea salt.

Swiss chard pie

Tourte de blettes

This is a speciality of Nice and dates back to 1393! It is an odd combination of sweetened chard and apple encased in pastry but, once tasted, is something that you will crave for the lovely combination of flavours.

Preparation: **40 minutes, plus 1 hour resting**

Cooking: **35 minutes**

Serves: **6**

Pastry

200g (7oz) plain flour

2 tsp baking powder

35g (scant 1½oz) caster sugar

pinch of salt

50g (2oz) butter, softened

1 egg, beaten

50ml (2fl oz) milk

Filling

50g (2oz) raisins

50g (2oz) pine nuts

100ml (3½fl oz) dark rum

10 large Swiss chard leaves

1 large dessert apple

grated zest of 1 lemon

2 tbsp apricot jam

60g (2¼oz) sugar

1 egg

25g (1oz) Parmesan cheese, grated

Preheat the oven to 200°C/400°F/Gas 6. Make the pastry: combine the flour, baking powder, sugar and salt in a bowl and rub in the butter until the mixture resembles breadcrumbs. Add the egg and milk, mix to form a ball, then wrap in cling film and place in the fridge to rest for 1 hour.

Soak the raisins and pine nuts in the rum. Blanch the Swiss chard leaves in boiling water for 2 minutes, then drain and squeeze out the excess water. Chop up the green leaves.

Grate the apple into a large bowl. Add the lemon zest, jam, sugar, egg, grated Parmesan, soaked pine nuts and raisins with the rum, and Swiss chard and mix well.

Cut the pastry in half. Lightly oil a 24cm (9½-inch) pie tin. Roll out one half of the pastry and use to line the tin base, pricking all over with a fork. Fill with the Swiss chard mixture, then roll out the remaining pastry and place on top of the pie. Pinch the edges to seal and prick with a fork. Bake for 35 minutes. Remove and leave to cool for 15 minutes, then serve.

Menton tart

Tarte de Menton

Menton is a town on the Riviera and its name is used for dishes inspired by the style of cooking in this area. This lovely tart is a staple and is always on Dominique's menu. For some reason, the onions and olives always taste sweeter in the south, making this a popular starter there.

Preparation: **40 minutes, plus 1 hour resting**

Cooking: **1 hour 5 minutes**

Serves: **6**

Pastry

150ml (¼ pint) milk

2 tsp baking powder

125g (4½oz) plain flour

pinch of salt

50ml (2fl oz) olive oil

Filling

3 large white onions, thinly sliced

2 tbsp olive oil

2 garlic cloves, chopped

1 bay leaf

sprig of fresh thyme

salt and freshly ground black pepper

125g (4½oz) black olives

Preheat the oven to 190°C/375°F/Gas 5. Warm the milk in a pan with the baking powder. Place the flour in a bowl, make a well in the middle and add the warm milk. Blend by hand, adding a pinch of salt and the olive oil, then kneading until smooth.

Roll out the pastry and use to line a well-oiled 24cm (9½-inch) tart tin. Cover with a cloth and leave to rest in the fridge for 1 hour.

For the filling, cook the onions slowly in the olive oil, add the garlic, herbs and seasoning, then cook gently for 15 minutes, without browning. Remove the herbs, then spread the onion mix on top of the pastry and bake for 30–35 minutes.

Remove the tart from the oven and lift out on to a rack. Scatter over the olives and serve at room temperature.

Index

Stuffed sardines

Sardines farcies

Nothing beats sea-fresh sardines and, with Dominique's unusual but tasty stuffing, this is a dish that is full of flavour.

Preparation: **25 minutes**
Cooking: **7–8 minutes**
Serves: **4**

125g (4½oz) crustless white bread
75ml (3fl oz) milk
50g (2oz) Swiss chard
125g (4½oz) smoked streaky bacon, minced
bunch of fresh parsley
1 shallot, roughly chopped
1 egg, beaten
50g (2oz) Parmesan cheese, grated
12 sardines, cleaned and boned
125g (4½oz) fresh breadcrumbs
lemon wedges, to serve

Preheat the oven to 200°C/400°F/Gas 6. Soak the bread in milk for 5 minutes. Blanch the Swiss chard for 2 minutes in boiling water, then drain and squeeze out any excess water.

Put the bacon, blanched Swiss chard, milk-soaked bread, parsley and shallot in a food processor and mix together. Add the egg and grated cheese.

Stuff the sardines with the stuffing mixture, then lightly roll the fish in breadcrumbs.

Place the stuffed sardines on a lightly oiled baking sheet and cook in the oven for 7–8 minutes. Serve with lemon wedges.